Delighting in God

A Key to Effective Spiritual Leadership

Gil Stieglitz

Delighting in God: A Key to Effective Spiritual Leadership

©2015 Gil Stieglitz
Published by Principles to Live By, Roseville CA 95661
www.ptlb.com

Cover by John Chase
Copyedited by Jennifer Edwards and Sandy Johnson

All rights reserved. No part of this publication may be reproduced, stored in a retrieval system, or transmitted in any way by any means—electronic, mechanical, photocopy, recording, or otherwise—without the prior permission of the copyright holder, except as provided by USA copyright law.

All Scripture verses are from the New American Standard Bible unless otherwise indicated. New American Standard Bible: 1995 update. 1995 La Habra, CA: The Lockman Foundation.

Due to the sensitive subject matter, names and other identifying information have been altered to protect the privacy of those whose stories and quotes are included in the book.

ISBN 978-0-9909641-2-4
Christian Living

Printed in the United States of America

Dedication

This book is dedicated to all the thousands of spiritual explorers down through the centuries who have learned to delight in God.

Table of Contents

Introduction...7

Delighting in God..25

Chapter 1: God in His Essence is Spirit......................27

Chapter 2: He is an Infinite Spirit..............................33

Chapter 3: He is an Infinite Self-Existent Spirit..........41

Chapter 4: His Attributes...53

Chapter 5: The Infinite, Self-Existent Spirit is Omniscient.........59

Chapter 6: The Infinite, Self-Existent Spirit is All Wise............75

Chapter 7: The Infinite, Self-Existent Spirit is Omnipotent........87

Chapter 8: The Infinite, Self-Existent Spirit is Omnipresent.....109

Chapter 9: The Infinite, Self-Existent Spirit is Immutable........119

Chapter 10: His Attributes: He is Holy............................137

Chapter 11: His Attributes: He is Righteous and Just.............157

Chapter 12: His Attributes: He is Good...........................175

Chapter 13: His Attributes: He is Sovereign......................185

Conclusion...211

About the Author...217

Delighting in God
Introduction

There is a danger in most discussions of spiritual warfare. It is the danger of talking way too much about the Devil and not enough about God. The greatest weapon (and really the only weapon) that the Christian has against the designs of the Devil is God Almighty. It is all that He says, does, and is that allows us to have any victory over the ravages of the devourer (1 Peter 5:8). I am hopeful that this little volume will put our focus where it should be in all issues of spiritual warfare: on God first and foremost.

The spiritual warrior needs to focus on the Lord God Almighty and not the Devil. The spiritual warrior has been invited into a relationship of delight and joy with the Ancient of Days. It is this relationship that must occupy his or her focus, not the evil that the Devil seduces people to commit. King David tells us that if we delight ourselves in the Lord, He will give us the desires of our heart (Psalm 37:4). If our desire is to release the captives from the snare of the Devil, then we should begin to delight in God at a higher level (2 Timothy 2:24-26).

Let me say this in a different way: The greatest way to defeat the devil and be liberated from the bondage of your past is to love God at a new depth. Jesus says in addressing the Father in John 17:3 that this is the eternal life: *to know you and Jesus Christ whom you have sent.* The power that is released when one pursues God and apprehends new aspects of His being pushes back the darkness. I have found that all relationships grow or fail based upon actions or inaction in five categories. Let me apply these to our relationship with God.

1. Are you acting in loving ways toward God? In our relationship with God we can't meet His needs, so we pursue Him and please Him to show Him that we love Him. We do that through practicing our faith through the spiritual disciplines.

2. How much immaturity is in your relationship with God? Are you behaving in mature or immature ways toward Him? In our relationship with God this means are we committing sins of omission, sins of commission, or sins of wickedness.

3. Are you growing in your understanding and acceptance of who God is? In our relationship with God we need to grow in our understanding of who God is and let Him increasingly be God in our life.

4. Does God occupy the proper place in your priorities? God's clear place in our priority structure is in first place. Is that where He is?

5. Are you willing to face the baggage of your past? In your relationship with God it increasingly becomes necessary to let God into every secret and every hurt so He can bring healing and truth. Each of these categories is important but in this book we will explore in depth the third relational category: Letting God be God in your life.

More loving pursuit of God	Mature behaviors toward God	Understanding, acceptance of who God is	Putting God in the proper priority order	Facing your past baggage
Usually through the Spiritual Disciplines	Eliminating Sins of Omission Sins of Commission Sins of Wickedness	Learning and making room for God to be God in your life	God is #1 Everything else comes after Him	Inviting God into your hurts, secrets, fears, struggles, programming, and dreams

There are many ways of delighting in God, but all of them start with learning and reveling in who God is and what He wants. Just as any other relationship of delight we may have, it is built on a growing understanding of our friend, beloved, or cherished mentor. Everything we need in life and our war with the Devil is contained in some aspect of God. Therefore what we need is God. We need to ask God, "What do I need to know of You and take delight in to move through this difficulty or season of my life?" I have known some people who have fallen in love with one attribute of God – like His love or His sovereignty or His power. They want to see everything that is happening and every answer to their life through that attribute of God. But that is naïve and limits God and, therefore, limits their growth in the abundant life Jesus came to give us. They often refuse to let God show them that He is so much more.

I can remember a man, let's call him Fred, who took great delight in the fact that God was righteous and would one day bring the wicked to judgment. Every time we would spend time praising God, Fred would loudly and emotionally proclaim his great delight that God would one day fry the wicked. He loved every lesson that talked about judgment day and God's righteous wrath. The Devil was devouring Fred and his whole family through Fred's lust for vengeance under the guise of delighting in the righteous wrath of God. I can remember the prayer time when it was clear that God was trying to get Fred's attention that He (God) was also loving. The solution to Fred's difficulty at that moment was God's love and grace to the people who had hurt him, but Fred wanted no part of forgiving and overlooking the hurts of the past. He wanted to see God's wrath consume those who had opposed him (Fred). His spiritual life just stopped and his family was being destroyed over his refusal to let God be loving.

I can also remember a man, let's call him Dave, who loved the fact that God was sovereign. God was in charge of everything. Everything that happened was just how God wanted it to happen. When God began emphasizing to Dave that He (God) was wisdom and knowledge, Dave didn't want any part of that revelation of God. If Dave had the opportunity to choose and he could change the nature of his relationships through his choices, then that meant that Dave was responsible for the lousy state of his marriage. It wasn't God's sovereignty; it was Dave's lack of wisdom. Dave refused to let God show him how his limited freedom of the will could truly change the nature of his marriage and his life. Dave had used God's sovereignty as a hammer for pushing for what he wanted in every situation. If it happened, then it became God's sovereign will and Dave was not responsible for what his selfishness produced. The Devil was devouring this man and his marriage through his narrow understanding of God. When Dave later opened up to the larger biblical understanding

Introduction

of all that God is and how God's wisdom, knowledge, goodness, grace, and love allow variability and choice within boundaries of God's sovereignty, then Dave was able to save his marriage.

I can remember a woman, let's call her Mary, who fell in love with the fact that God was loving, good, gracious, and merciful. All she wanted to know about God was His forgiveness and His mercy. Mary refused to embrace anything about God being righteous, sovereign, omnipotent, and all knowing. The Bible said that God was love and that was all she ever wanted to know about God (1 John 4:8). Over time her singular understanding of God as only a God of love moved her to begin worshipping a weak and impotent God who would fix things in this world but just wasn't allowed or powerful enough. I can remember, after a national tragedy in which hundreds of people died because of the evil of a few people, I preached a message about where was God in that tragedy and why had God allowed it. Mary angrily came up to me after the service and told me in no uncertain terms that her God would not allow that type of tragedy and had nothing to do with it. I remember gently but firmly saying, "I know that your god would not allow this tragedy, but your god does not exist and the real God did allow this and we must come to understand why. You must grow in your understanding and worship of God, or you will soon be worshipping a god of your own invention." We don't get to make God any way we want. The God of the Bible exists, and we are to enter into a relationship of delight with the fullness of God or at some point our spiritual growth will stop because of our stubborn refusal to let God be God.

I have regularly found that in my time of worship and prayer, I approach God from a particular attribute or aspect of His being and God redirects me through the Scriptures to another aspect of His being that is exactly what I need to know and delight in with Him in order to solve the situations or dilemmas of my life at that time. Sometimes I want to limit God to my favorite attributes or my favorite promises, and there is no help from God in those directions. I must allow God to use the whole Scriptures to let me know who He is. When I free God up to teach me through the whole Scriptures who He is, then I can be in a relationship of delight. I do not always like what God shows me in the Scripture about the solution to my situation or some aspect of His being, but my relationship with the Lord God Almighty can continue. Think of Abraham and his interactions with God and how he needed to constantly be open to new levels and new ideas as he had discussions with God about Sodom, about Lot, about Egypt. Think about the Apostle Peter being stretched by God to embrace His love for the Gentiles (Acts 10). Think about the Apostle Paul having his mind blown by the appearance of Jesus as God in the vision that changed his whole life. If you are going to have a growing relationship with God, then your understanding and relationship with Him must grow past your original Sunday School understanding of Him.

It is time to take delight in God, with God, about God, and for God. Only as God becomes our focus will we be able to defeat the Devil. The Devil is a devourer (1 Peter 5:8), but God gives life. The more we know about Him and take delight in Him, the more we can enjoy the incredible life that He wants to give us (John 10:10). The Devil is the mold committee that destroys the souls of those who turn in a selfish direction. God is the source of all life and redeems souls who were destined to be devoured but instead turned to Him and asked Him to save them. Put your focus on God. Find your answers in Him. Look to Him. Yes, we must be alert to the Devil and his schemes to turn us to selfishness and sin but keep your eyes fixed on Jesus the author and perfecter of the faith (Heb. 12:2).

The Devil will try and hide the wonder of God from you. He will try and lie to you about what God is like and why He is doing what He is doing. This is why it is important if you are to grow spiritually and have a relationship of delight with God. Your understanding of God must grow. You must know what God is and what God will never do. For the Devil will try to deceive you about why certain things are happening and what this means about God. Do not let the Devil's lies warp your Christian life. Grow in your delight in the knowledge and grace of the Lord Jesus Christ (2 Peter 3:18).

Let me suggest four different ways to increase your delight in God. You can do them at the same time or space them out over the course of a year or dedicate a month (for example: September) every year to expanding your understanding of God through the use of one of these plans

First, read and contemplate the wonder of God in the spiritual exercises of this book, *Delighting in God: A Key to Effective Spiritual Leadership*. Each day read through the pages about who God is and do the exercise that is attached to it. Record your new insights into God so that you will have a record of your growth in this crucial practice of delighting in God.

Second, read five Psalms every day, asking God to show you what you need to know about Him or your situation to handle it righteously? You can read five Psalms in a row or you can read the Psalm that corresponds to whatever day it is today, adding 30 four more times until you have read five Psalms. If for instance today is the 15 of the month, then read the 15th Psalm, then the 45th Psalm, then the 75th Psalm, then the 105th Psalm, and finally the 135th Psalm. In this way you will read through all 150 Psalms in a month and allow God to guide you to a much deeper understanding of who He is from Scripture.

Again, write down the verses that God highlighted and read those verses at various times through the day and meditate upon these spiritual truths about God and the Christian life.

Third, use the praise guide, *Touching the Face of God*, to go on a 40-day adventure into the wonder of God. This is designed to take you scriptually and prayerfully through all the aspects of God's being. This will allow God to speak to your soul about aspects of His being that you may have been neglecting.

Fourth, read through a good theological book on God. I would recommend, *Knowing God* by J.I. Packer or *Knowledge of the Holy* by A.W. Tozer. As you read along in the book, look up the verses and contemplate the wonder of God. Pray to God about your expanded understanding of who He is and what He is doing.

Introduction

What is the main purpose of human existence?

To delight in God and to glorify Him forever.
(Psalm 37:4; John 17:3; Colossians 2:17,23)

The purpose of human existence is first and foremost to delight in God (to know Him, to enjoy Him, to wait upon Him). We were made to have a relationship with God, and we will not fully be able to comprehend life until we have that relationship. Delighting in God is finding our delight in the actual person of God. Nothing else will satisfy the human condition. We were designed and made by God with the unique ability to know intimacy with God Almighty.

There is a rumor going around that there is more to the Christian life than the typical present version of it that is offered in the average church. These rumors appear in the Scripture and in the true saints down through the centuries. The Apostle John speaks of it when he says that there is a third stage to the Christian life where a Christian is intimately acquainted with the One who was from the beginning. Jesus speaks of it when He says, "This is the eternal life, to know God and Jesus Christ whom You have sent." The Apostle Paul speaks of it when he says, "He counts all things to be loss in view of the surpassing value of knowing Christ Jesus our Lord." David, the sweet singer of Israel, speaks of it when he calls his fellow Israelites to delight in the Lord and all their desires will come true. Isaiah the prophet speaks of it in the lofty section on God when he says, "Wait upon the Lord."

There is more, so much more. There will always be more to know, more to delight in, more to be enraptured with; but you must chose to go down that path. You must turn away from the baubles and temptations of this world. Seek the Lord and His righteousness. Survival in the world we live in depends upon a deeper understanding of God in some aspect of His being. It is possible to become so confused by the choices of the world that we make a foolish decision to pursue something that cannot last. I have found that when I am weighed down by the cares of this world, I can approach God and begin to delight in Him, and He will direct me to that aspect of His being which I need to be reminded of or which instructs me how to act. And I am in a different place after that encounter with God.

There are times when I need to be reminded that God is longsuffering and He asks me to be faithful and longsuffering with people. There are times when I need God to tell me that He is all knowing and all wise and in that way goad me to search harder for the wisdom I need to escape the difficulty I am in. There are times when I need to know that God is sovereign and He has not forgotten me, but I am walking out a part of His plan even though at the time I am tempted to cut and run. Sometimes I need to be reminded of how much God has expressed His love already, so I will stop whining about some present petty difficulty.

When I am the most tempted or afflicted, I need to spend time with God the Almighty. I need Him to teach me about Himself and strengthen me to live this life with His power, His energy, His love, and His wisdom. We need to delight in God and have Him teach us about Himself through the Scriptures. When God speaks out of the Scriptures and speaks directly to your heart about the truth of who He is, then you are energized to change.

We are in a constant war with temptation, the world's values, and fear to abandon the righteous path. This is what spiritual warfare is all about. But delighting in God the Almighty and having Him reveal Himself to your soul is the most powerful weapon of all. Satan is not the winner; he is a collector of losers. God the Almighty is the winner, and He is collecting a group of people who delight in Him so that He can delight in them. God has consistently told us in the Scriptures that there are four aspects to His being: His Essence, His Attributes, His Nature, and His Names (space does not permit us to do a deep dive into the Names of God in this volume). If we are going to delight in Him, then it will be these Scriptural revelations about God that we will focus on to start our deeper dive into the wonder of God.

This is very important to embrace. The goal of life is not church or good deeds; it is delighting in God and glorifying Him. Church becomes an irrelevant obstacle if it does not introduce us to this soul-satisfying relationship with God. What does He want you to do? What is He revealing about Himself? What is He revealing about you?

Do you have a relationship of delight with God the Almighty?

The beginning of every ancient discipleship program sought to answer the big questions right up front. There was no need to shy away from the fundamental questions about human existence because Christianity has the answers. What is the purpose of human existence? Why is there evil in the world? Where is God? Who is God? What is man? How did man come to be? These are the questions that modern man is asking and is receiving no answers. When modern culture cut itself off from the Living God and the truth about Him, it eliminated any coherent answers to the really big questions of life. When we reject the Living God, there are no answers on a personal, national, or cultural level. All that is left is a series of experiments in futility: Hedonism, Statism, Stoicism, Naturalism, Rationalism, Communism, Postmodernism, etc.

How do we come to delight in God?

1. God sends His grace (Ephesians 2:8,9) to call, convict, illuminate, draw (John 6:44), and enable us.

It is important to realize that God is always the initiator in any relationship with Himself. The Bible makes clear that humans are unable – in their present sinful condition – to initiate anything in God's direction (Romans 5:8; John 15:5). God in His love and mercy has paid the penalty of our rebellion and initiated its application to our condition (2 Corinthians 5:19,21).

2. We begin to delight in God by entering into and sustaining a personal relationship with Him (John 1:12; 17:3; Matthew 7:21-23; 1 John 1:3).

We become aware of all the work that God has done and is doing to initiate and enable this soul-satisfying relationship with Him when He calls to our soul (Hebrews 3:7,15). We must not resist this call but instead embrace this divine work and the answers that it brings.

Faith is the means through which this relationship with God is received, transacted, and maintained. We are empowered by God to trust in Him. Our embrace of His grace through faith allows the journey of delight to begin.

3. We begin to delight in God by gaining intellectual and personal understanding of God's being (Psalm 50:21, John 6:29) and His major works (Genesis 1:1-2:3; Psalm 19:1-4; Romans 1:18-20).

All of the above aspects of knowing God must be kept in front of the truly Christian disciple. One must grow in their understanding of the God who is, so that they do not begin to worship or serve a god of their own invention. Also, it is not enough to just know accurately about the one True and Living God; one must enter into and then maintain a personal relationship with the Almighty God. It is important that the disciple keep pursuing the Holy God personally at the same time they are allowing their understanding of God to grow in an objective sense.

How do we glorify God?

The ultimate purpose for living is to delight in God and to glorify Him. Therefore the obvious question is: How does one adequately glorify the Almighty God with their life?

First, a person glorifies God by bringing their life into conformity with His will. This means that negatively they stay within the boundaries of the Ten Commandments (Exodus 20:1-17). Positively it means that the believer acts like Christ in every situation they find themselves (Matthew 5:3-12; Galatians 5:22,23). And subjectively, they remain alert and obedient to the gentle prompting of the Holy Spirit (Jeremiah 31:33, Romans 8:14; Ephesians 5:18; Isaiah 20:20,21).

Secondly, a believer glorifies God by using the talents, gifts, abilities, and dreams that God has given them to their fullest, righteous potential (Luke 19:12-27; Colossians 3:23).

In other words, the reason for my existence is to have a relationship of delight with God and glorify Him through maximizing my talents, gifts, abilities, and dreams righteously within the boundaries of His commandments. Living life at God's direction is a delightful life. He has made us to glorify Him by doing certain things, having specific relationships, and becoming particular kinds of

Introduction

people. Grow into all that He hoped you would be and take delight in Him as you do it.

How do we begin?

Oh Lord, I want to delight in You. I want to contemplate the wonder of your being. I want to praise the glory of your existence. I want to know You more than I do. I want to have my mind shaped by the truths of who You are. Show me the aspects of Your being that I need to pursue at this point in my life.

Take the tables and pray that God will show you the area(s) that you need to explore to bring new levels of delight to your relationship with God.

Aspect	Verses	Definition
His Essence		
Infinite	Genesis 213:3; Isaiah 45:5-7	God has always existed and will always exist.
Self-Existent	Acts 17:24,25; Exodus 3:14	God is life itself and does not need us.
Spirit	John 4:24; Luke 24:39	God is alive, invisible, is a person, and has no body.

Aspect	Verses	Definition
His Attributes		
The non-moral attributes		These are the non-moral attributes. They have the least connection with us as humans and are very unlike us.
Omniscient	Romans 16:27; Job 21:22; 1 Samuel 2:3	God is all knowing and all wise.
Omnipotent	Revelation 19:6; Luke 1:37; Psalm 147:5	God has all power and all authority to do whatever is consistent with His nature.
Omnipresent	Psalm 139:7-12; Jer. 23:24,25	God is everywhere present.
Immutable	Malachi 3:6; James 1:17; Hebrews 13:8	God does not change.

Aspect	Verses	Definition
His Attributes		
The moral attributes		These are the moral attributes. Some would understand that our limited capacity for these attributes is a part of the image of God in man.
Holiness	1 Peter 1:15,16; Job 34:10; Leviticus 19:2; Isaiah 6:1-3	God is transcendent and pure.
Goodness	Exodus 34:6,7; Psalm 34:8-10; James 1:17; Deut. 30:9	God is loving, gracious, merciful, and longsuffering.
Righteous	Galatians 6:7; Psalm 58:11; Romans 2:7; Romans 1:18; Romans 2:5,6	God always does what is right; rewards and punishes according to righteous standards.
Sovereign	1 Chronicles 29:11; Daniel 4:35; Ephesians 1:11; Ezekiel 18:4	God is in control preserving, directing, and containing.

Most people are fascinated by God but few are in relationship with Him. Even fewer of those who have embraced His gift of grace in His Son regularly push into His presence and enjoy deep fellowship. But God invites us through the apostles (1 John 1:1-3) to have our sins forgiven and a secure place in heaven. Come and learn how to praise God while learning about Him. This work has been thirty years in the making. I have used these praise exercises with all kinds of people over the years, and the result is always the same – a deeper understanding of God and entrance into the joy of His presence. Each time I practice these exercises – whether individually or in a group – it is as C.S. Lewis writes in his *Chronicles of Narnia*... "Further up and further in." There is nothing like pushing into the presence of God.

Delighting in God

Begin by just reciting a prayer of trust in God that is familiar to many of you: Psalm 23. Slowly read this Psalm out loud three times today. Ask God how He is trying to do these actions in your life. Let Him give you a new perspective on some of the people, work, and situations that are in your life. Ask the Lord how you are resisting Him in what He is trying to do. Let the Lord bring up areas where He is pointing out a really good path to take, but you are resisting because it isn't cool or doesn't seem prestigious enough or some other excuse.

> *The LORD is my shepherd, I shall not want. He makes me lie down in green pastures;*
> *He leads me beside quiet waters.*
> *He restores my soul;*
> *He guides me in the paths of righteousness for His name's sake.*
> *Even though I walk through the valley of the shadow of death,*
> *I fear no evil, for You are with me;*
> *Your rod and Your staff, they comfort me.*
> *You prepare a table before me in the presence of my enemies;*
> *You have anointed my head with oil;*
> *My cup overflows.*
> *Surely goodness and lovingkindness will follow me all the days of my life,*
> *And I will dwell in the house of the LORD forever.*

Where is God right now making you lie down where you don't really want to lie down? It is a good place but not your preferred place. He is blessing you but you can think of something you want more, so you are restless and rebellious with your present assignment.

Where is your soul in need of restoration? Are you resisting the people, activities, or process that are designed by God to restore your soul? Are you wanting a quick charge so you can go charge ahead again and yet God seems to want to give you a trickle charge?

Are you right now aware that He is guiding your paths of righteousness but the paths of sin and selfishness seem more exciting? What is the temptation wanting you to do? What is God doing to keep you in the path of righteousness?

Are you walking through a very scary place right now? Does it seem like you have no real safety net except God? How is He protecting you? Is He prompting you to take precautions you don't want to take? Is He sending people or rules your way to help you get through this scary time?

Who are the enemies who have sought to hold you down or remove you? What is God doing right now that could lead to your being honored with them – being forced to watch or participate?

Chapter 1
God in His Essence is Spirit

John 4:24 - *God is spirit, and those who worship Him must worship in spirit and truth.*

Jesus tells us that the essential essence of God is Spirit. This means that He does not have a body or spatial dimensions (Luke 24:39). He is invisible and cannot be seen in our limited dimensions of space and time (Deuteronomy 4:15-19; Romans 1:20, Colossians 1:15; 1 Timothy 1:17). The Bible tells us that no man has seen God or can see Him (1 Timothy 6:16). He needed to explain Himself into our limited dimensional universe, so the Son of God took on flesh and became the perfect expression of the invisible God in this world (Colossians 1:15; Hebrews 1:1-3). Certain Scriptures indicate that one day we will be changed from this mortal flesh so that we will "see" Him (Psalm 17:15; Matthew 5:8; Hebrews 12:14; Revelations 22:4).

Someone might object that God describes himself as having eyes, hands, and even feet in various passages (Isaiah 68:21; Genesis 3:8, I Kings 8). Yes, the Bible does use these expressions about God, but all of these expressions are anthropomorphic. God is explaining Himself and His actions in ways we can understand. He uses terms and metaphors that we use all the time to help us understand His person and being. A spirit does not have these physical parts.

When Jesus declares that God is Spirit, it also means that He is alive (Joshua 3:10). He is not static or inanimate or pure energy. He is alive in that He thinks, feels, moves, decides, and acts. He is called the Living God (Samuel 17:26; Psalm 84:21; Matthew 16:16; I Thessalonians 1:9). He is Himself the source of all life (Acts 17:28; 1 John 5:26, Psalm 36:9).

What else does it mean when Jesus declares that God is Spirit? It means that God is a person (Exodus 3:14). He is not a law or a principle or a singularity. He is an individual unity from which all things flow – not necessarily but voluntarily – because He wills it. It is not possible to have an impersonal spirit for this denies the self-consciousness and self-determination implied in the concept spirit. God is self-conscious (Isaiah 45:5, I Corinthians 2:10). God is self-determined (Job 23:13, Romans 9:11, Hebrews 6:17).

How do I use the truth that God is Spirit to take delight in Him? (What does it mean to us that God is spirit?)

1. I can delight in moving beyond a simplistic Sunday School understanding of God. He is not Santa Claus in the heavens doling out presents reluctantly if people pray right. He is not a genie in heaven waiting to grant people three wishes. He is not a vending machine in the sky waiting for people to put in the right amount of coins. He is a person who thinks, feels, loves, plans, decides, and wants a real relationship with each of us individually. Yes, He gives gifts and blessings but He is so much more. He is a person. Through Jesus Christ's death He offers the real relationship with Himself. This is amazing and delightful.

2. I take delight in the fact that God is invisible and is not confined to a body. He is always available to me. He is never too busy for me or occupied on another matter. He cannot die and is not held up in any part of this universe. I know that He cannot be adequately rendered or worshipped in a picture or statue (Isaiah 40:18-20). In fact, God forbids this practice or type of worship (Exodus 20:4,5, Deuteronomy 4:12). I know that the Devil will try and deceive me into representing God in some three-dimensional way and then bowing down to that image or statute and in this way rob me in some measure of my relationship with the real God who is above, beyond, before, and everywhere present. I take delight in the invisible Living God.

3. I take delight in the fact that the invisible God did not stay hidden but showed Himself through His actions, attributes, and self-revelation in the Scriptures and in the Lord Jesus Christ. He could have remained hidden, leaving us wandering in the dark about who He is and what He is like; but He told us and showed us because He wants us to have a relationship with Him (John 14:5-7, Hebrews 1:3). Do not let the Devil lie to you that the invisibility of God means He is a figment of your imagination. He is real and the Devil knows that. The Devil also knows that we, through our bodies, are partial to three-dimensional realities. This is why God gave us the Lord Jesus.

4. I take delight in the fact that God desires spiritual worship (John 4:23,24). The worship that pleases God is when our innermost being celebrates the work and wonder of God. He is not more pleased with our worship when the buildings, voices, and clothes are the most beautiful. He wants the authentic spiritual worship that comes from the core of your soul, not when we make trappings and masks. A dirt floor in a mud hut is just as wonderful of a house of worship as a grand cathedral. Do not let the Devil convince you that you are not worthy of worshipping the Almighty. Take it by faith that you are not worthy, but God qualifies us through His Son Jesus Christ. God desires spiritual and true worship, not perfect worship or wealthy worship. Worship God the Almighty, Creator of all the World.

5. I take delight in my God that He is incapable of being hurt by physical force (Acts 5:29, Nahum 1:9, Psalm 2:3,4). There is no physical army or empire that will one day overthrow God. He sits as King over the whole world from beginning to end. All other empires and dynasties grow weary and bureaucratic but not the Kingdom of God. He cannot be conquered by an earthly power.

6. I take delight in God that He communicates with us, spirit to spirit (Romans 8:14). He is a person and wants to relate to us. This is amazing. He has not left us alone on a spinning rocket ship but has reached out and continues to reach out to us individually and collectively. We must become more well-versed in His written love letters. We must also become sensitive to the still small voice of the Lord (1 Kings 19:11-14, Jeremiah 31:33,34). I take great delight in the truth that He can and will lead us (Romans 8:14), guide us (Psalm 31:3; John 16:13), teach us (John 14:26), convict us (I Corinthians 4:3,5), give us gifts and blessings (1 Corinthians 12:7; James 1:17), empower us (Acts 1:8), and many other wonders. These are all forms of communication with us.

7. I take great delight in the fact that He primarily blesses us with the highest of His blessings: spiritual blessings (Ephesians 1:3). We are half physical and half spiritual creatures, and we can be duped into believing that the physical blessings of money, shelter, food, prestige, and power are better than the spiritual blessings of love, joy, truth, humility, peace, forgiveness, justice, responsibility, and righteousness. This is the Devil's delight to deceive us into selling our spiritual blessings for physical trophies that can't last. But the spiritual ones are far better. If we have the physical blessings without the spiritual ones, we are miserable. But if we have the spiritual blessings without the physical ones, our soul still has a feast. Because God is a spirit and He loves us, He is trying to get us to embrace the spiritual blessings He is giving. Yes, He does give us physical blessings. We must not make the mistake of valuing the material higher than the spiritual.

8. I take delight in God being a spirit who wants to be in a growing relationship with me. Any two persons who are in a relationship must have that relationship grow or it begins to die. The relationship that I had with God in the beginning of my spiritual journey is not as good as it gets. It can get deeper, richer, more intense, more enjoyable, and more based upon knowledge and shared experiences (Matthew 23:37, Jeremiah 29:12,13; John 17:3). One must spend time pursuing Him and must practice certain basic relational disciplines or the intimacy of the interaction will break down. It is important to pursue Him and want to learn more about Him so you can have a growing relationship of delight with Him. What does He want you to do with all the arenas of your life? What does He think and feel about world events? What injustices need to be righted from His point of view?

I have drawn some obvious applications that can spur your relationship with God forward into new levels of joy. You may also make more applications that are based upon Scripture.

How is God as a Spirit to be differentiated from other spirits (such as angels, demons, or the human spirit)?

God is an Infinite, Self-Existent Spirit. This is how the Bible describes God at the core of His essence. All other spirits are finite and dependent.

Chapter 2
God's Essence:
He is an Infinite Spirit

God is eternal and has no beginning or end. He existed before the beginning of our universe, and He will exist after this universe is changed (Revelations 21). God is infinite in regard to time (eternity) and space (immense). He is outside of our time dimensions. He does not age nor die. His perspective is beyond our comprehension. At one point in Abraham's spiritual journey he was introduced to the infinitude of God (Genesis 21:33). He, as a spiritual explorer, begins to interact with God as the Everlasting One. He saw that there was so much more than his life. God who was his friend was so much greater and so much more dynamic than he (Abraham) had ever contemplated.

Contemplate that as vast as our universe is, God is above, beyond, before, and after it. God created our universe and its space and time. God invented atoms and natural laws. He invented space and planned its existence. There was some debate for centuries whether the universe we dwell in is eternal. But that has been proven to be an invalid conclusion and almost all scientists embrace the fact that the universe sprang into existence out of nothing. It is only God who is eternal without beginning or end (Psalm 90:2, 102:27, Isaiah 57:15, I Timothy 6:18). He surrounds time as a sheet of paper surrounds the line which is drawn on it. God the Almighty was before the first atom, before the first ray of light, before time, before space. Not only did God exist before all of space and time, but the Scriptures tell us that He planned our existence and knew all the possibilities of all the possibilities of everything that would or could happen (Romans 8:29; Matthew 11:20-24). After our sun goes super nova, God will still exist and will still be God.

Also realize that He is infinite in terms of space. He is immense in that He is not confined to any one place but fills the earth and the heavens (I Kings 8:27, Jeremiah 23:24). He fills all space but is separate from His creation – it not being a part of Him nor He dwelling in it (Genesis 1:12,18, Matthew 10:29, John 1:12). He is in every place, but He is not in everything.

Pray the following prayer in dialogue and delight with the Infinite God. Pause after each of the questions in this prayer and listen for God's response in your soul. I think you will be amazed at the dialogue you will begin with the Everlasting God.

Oh God, You are the everlasting infinite God. Your perspective is clear having watched and known thousands of people down through the centuries. There are mistakes that I am about to make that if I just listened to You a whole new aspect of my life would open up. I want to know You as the everlasting God. So often I live my life without your everlasting perspective. Many times I need to slow down and see things from a longer point of view; Your point of view. Show me where my hurry and short-term thinking is destroying the relational life You want me to have. Help me, grow me, and change me to see as You see.

He is an Infinite Spirit

Where do I see things from a short-term perspective? What do I need to do to be in step with Your long-term will for me?

Where am I so busy about things that will not last? Lord, what am I worrying about that in heaven a thousand years from now I will be amazed that it even concerned me?

Lord, what do I really need to be concerned about that is coming ten years from now or thirty years from now that I tend to put aside because of my short-term perspective?

Oh Lord, what is happening in my world that is really just a repeat of something that has happened before. You are the Ancient of Days; what should concern me about the choices of my family, my community, and my nation?

Let God speak to you from out of His infinity so that you might delight in His infinite perspective.

How do I take delight in the infinitude of God?

1. I can take delight in the fact that God sees everything – both good or bad – personally and does not need to hear a report. I do not have to worry if someone else will pray first and persuade God that I was wrong and they were right. He was there and knows exactly what happened. I also can take delight in God that when I do some hidden good deed, He is there to see it. I do not have to brag about what I have done because the one person who needs to know already knows. He is personally aware of every sinful detail and every virtuous action or thought (I Proverbs 16:3). I can talk with God about a situation, person, or activity as someone who was there. He does not need me to inform Him of what happened. In fact, many times in prayer He can let me know other perspectives about the situation that I am unaware of. God knows everything about me and still wants to be in a relationship with me. The Devil can play up how unworthy you are and all your hidden sins, but you now know that God knows them all and still pursued you for a relationship of blessing, love, and joy.

2. I can marvel and take delight in the fact that God Almighty is beyond my finite mind's ability to understand Him. We will never fully comprehend Him or exhaust His person with our rational categories (Isaiah 40:16, Psalm 90:2). We understand that what we can understand about God is some infinitesimally small amount of all that the Transcendent God is really all about. God is infinite in every sense of that word. When we contemplate the wonder of all that He knows just to set up the laws, biology, geology, thermodynamics, and physics of this universe, we are overwhelmed. And clearly God knows more and is more than just the Creator of this universe. Marvel at Him and the fact that this infinite God wants to guide you in your daily life (Isaiah 30:21; Romans 8:14).

3. I can take great joy in what is revealed in Scriptures that Christians have an infinite inheritance beyond time and space. God, the Infinite Spirit, is infinitely filling, infinitely satisfactory, infinitely pleasant (Psalm 16:11; 1 Corinthians 2:9). Imagine what is in store for God's faithful servants when their leader is infinitely creative and infinitely loving. Too many people have heard heaven depicted as a static place that seems boring, but we serve an infinitely creative God who is storing up a great inheritance for us. When you think of heaven, think of the infinite creativity that is displayed in the creation itself. This is the kind of God that we serve and who will be rewarding us with Himself and an infinite variety of people, places, service, and joy (Revelation 22:1-10).

4. I can take delight that God sees everything and will reward what is done in secret and not for the praise of men. We can work in secret without external recognition because we know that God sees and will ultimately reward (Matthew 6:4,6,18). God takes special delight when we, His children, do good works in secret counting on His eyes seeing it but no one else. We do not have to get the praise of men because we know that God is watching everything and will reward us in this life and the life to come for every good deed we do (even though He was the one who prompted it, energized it, and set up the opportunity).

5. Because God is infinite I can continue my relationship with God anywhere that I am. In prison, in an airplane, in a crowded room, in a church service – all of these places and every other place you can think of one can have a relationship with the Almighty. He truly is with you unto the end of the age (Matthew 28:20). The Christian can continue his relationship with God no matter where he is because God is there (Acts 17:27, Hebrews 11:27, Genesis 5:21). We are not hampered by location or lack of a temple or building. I can ask God for help, guidance, and mercy wherever I find myself. Even if I have run far away from Him and am in a morally bad place, I can access the infinite God because He is there hoping I would change my mind and return to Him. Never let the Devil tell you that you have done too many bad things, so you can't return to God. I had the privilege of leading my grandfather to the forgiveness that is in Jesus Christ. The Devil had kept him in prison with this lie for years. Yes, he had done many selfish, sinful, and even criminal things but there was forgiveness in Jesus Christ. Twelve hours before he died he knelt by his bedside and prayed a prayer asking for forgiveness from the God his grandson told him about. He begged for forgiveness, and I know that the Lord Jesus was ready to give it to him. How tragic that he waited till right before he died to gain the forgiveness that was waiting for him all his life.

6. I can take delight in the immensity of God's infinitude. Too often we allow our own limitations to transfer to God. Whatever situation or problem you are in, God knows the solution. Christians must not limit their understanding of what God can do (Romans 11:33). Think through what this means. He has an answer. He has a way through. He can see what you cannot see. An obstacle to us is not an obstacle to Him. We may see only one way of solving a problem, but He can move in dimensions and directions which we do not understand. God is not limited by our categories. The Devil will try and convince you that because there is some theological or moral problem you or others can't solve, it means that God must not exist. This is ridiculous. God is infinite.

7. I can take delight in the infinitude of God in that He surrounds time like one brush stroke is surrounded by the whole of the painting. He is the ever-present one. We can pray for an event that is past tense to us but remains unknown in its outcome. God can apply it to the past. I have many times told someone that I would pray for them because of a surgery or difficult situation and yet I have forgotten. I remember after the surgery or the specific time has occurred. If I do not know how it turned out, I will pray anyway asking God to apply my prayer to the event that was in the past but unknown to me. This would not be appropriate for events that we know the outcome already. God will not change the timeline after the fact but because He is infinite, He can receive our prayers about an event that is unknown to us as though they happened before the event was settled.

8. Because God is infinite, I can take the delightful assignment of looking at how He has acted in the past in my life and trace His grace and mercy into the future. Too many times we only look at the past from our own perspectives, but I have watched people's whole world open up when they allowed God to show them a different view of their childhood or first marriage. We can reexamine a past event looking for evidence of God's presence and direction. If a person is willing to let God show you how He was there in your life in the past, He will show you (James 1:5). His grace was present. His mercy was active. Yes, evil is and was possible and God does not remove the power of choice from His creatures, but it is clear that He was present there in that awful period and wants to show you how to see that time with new eyes and redeem it in new ways (Romans 8:28,29).

9. One of the delightful things about the infinite God is that He is working an infinite plan. I am part of that plan. Let your mind realize that God has planned the universe we live in and the planet we live on as well as our lives. He has designed into our existence the possibility of good works that will fulfill you and bless you (Ephesians 2:10). God is also moving you to link up with a part of His plan that He started dozens or hundreds of years ago. I know that I am one of the answers to prayer of my great aunt. Over a hundred years ago now my grandfather rebelled from the Christian upbringing that he was given. He pursued drink, women, money, and sloth. His sister, my great aunt, began praying for my grandfather even though he was spitting blasphemes at God. She also prayed that a preacher would come out of his heirs to redeem the damage that he (my grandfather) was doing. God clearly listened to the prayers of my great aunt and called me to repentance and to the ministry of preaching the Word. He moved in answer to prayer and the fifty to one hundred years it took was no problem to Him. God can move two or more people to accomplish His purpose. Even though they are separated by thousands of miles or thousands of years, He is there and can work there. Do not let the Devil rob you of trust in God just because the answer to your prayer did not happen quick enough.

Chapter 3
God's Essence: He is an Infinite Self-Existent Spirit

Acts 17:24,25 - *The God who made the world and all things in it, since He is Lord of heaven and earth, does not dwell in temples made with hands; nor is He served by human hands, as though He needed anything, since He Himself gives to all people life and breath and all things.*

The Self-Existence of God

This verse in the New Testament is one of the clearest examples of what is called the self-existence of God. God is life itself. He does not have life. He is life. Everything else derives its level of life and living from Him. He is the generator of this thing we call life. It is very important to realize that nothing gave Him life. He is life. There is no outside source that started God or that periodically comes by and re-energizes God. NO, God is the Supreme God who is life in Himself. Any aspect of His being is life. It is why the Apostle John could say that He is the Life. It is how God could reveal to Moses that His name is I AM. He is ultimately what it means to be.

Notice the phrase in Acts 17:25 - *He is not served by human hands, as though He needed anything.* This is a very important phrase that is the conclusion of the apostle's understanding of the Old Testament. It is clear that for God to be the Supreme God, He cannot be dependent on His creation. It is amazing that God, who is life itself, wants to share His life with us. We have scientists looking all over the solar system for the source of life and it is God. He wants to invite us into the very life that His character and being generates. He wants us to enjoy direct connection to His self-sufficiency. He invites us past the angels, past the creation, past the animals, and past every other being into His presence. He wants us to plug into Him, who is life (John 1:4; 1 John 1:2). What will it feel like when in heaven we access directly the source of all life?

Notice the phrase, *"He Himself gives life to all people life and breath and all things."* Everything comes from Him and nothing flows back in the other direction. He is life and it flows from Him outward. Grasp this... the all-sufficient God who needs nothing and cannot be served by humanity, creates the universe and this world so that He can show His love to completely unworthy creatures and invite those creatures into fellowship with Him. This is mind-blowing. Too often we fall into the trap of believing that we are something special as humans or as individuals. We believe that it is obvious why God would want a relationship with us. But it is not obvious when you really contemplate the truth about God. There is no reason that God would ever mess with us. But His love for us compels Him to reach out to us. When was the last time you reached out to care for someone who would in no way benefit you? When was the last time you were

He is an Infinite Self-Existent Spirit

willing to alter your whole life to care for a person, animal, or thing that disrespected you and didn't appreciate what you were doing?

What does it mean to say that God is self-existent?

It means that He does not need anything from us. He did not create the world because He was lonely or because He wanted more worship. He was perfectly self-sufficient and content in the Trinity (Father, Son, and Holy Spirit) loving and being loved. We need Him but He does not need us. This makes it all the more remarkable that He loves us. He understands and meets our needs even at great personal cost to Himself (the sacrifice of His only begotten Son). He pursues us when we are not pursuing Him (Romans 5:8). He pleases us with good things that are beyond our needs (James 1:17).

It means that we cannot love Him as He can love us. We can please Him and pursue Him, but we cannot meet any needs that He may or may not have. To love in a biblical sense means to meet needs, to pursue, and/or to please. We cannot meet any needs God has – if He has any. So that form of love which is the most common form of love is not available to us in relation to God. But we can pursue Him as an act of love. We can seek Him with all our heart. We can try and please Him. We will never be on equal footing with the Almighty Self-existent God in that He has no needs that we can meet. But He does accept our feeble pursuit of Him as love. He accepts our attempts to do His commands and to please Him as love. He invites us to love Him in these ways.

Any needs that God has are completely met within the Tri-une oneness of the Father, Son, and the Holy Spirit (Matthew 28:18-20; John 17:21-24). He is completely self-contained. One of the wonders of the Trinity of God is that it clearly backs up the self-sufficiency of God. Some have argued that if the true God is love, then He needed to create in order to have something outside of Himself to love. This is not true because God is not a singularity only. He is a tri-unity. He is and was completely contented in the Trinity loving and being loved. He did not need to create the universe or angels or humanity to have something to love. He did choose to create and love us, but it did not grow out of any need He had. He is truly self-sufficient. He is complete and content within Himself: Father, Son, and Holy Spirit.

Praise God that He never needs anything from any human. For what if He needed something from a human and that human did not do it? Praise God that He is above, beyond, and over every human and angelic personage. He is God -- the self-sufficient One. We draw close to God when we admit that we need Him. We worship Him when we acknowledge all the ways that we specifically need Him. Take some time and write out or pray out how you need God in your life. Where do you need Him to come through? Cry out to God about the information, the miracles, the finances, the relationships, the direction, the opportunities that you need to move your life forward. Ask Him for those things, always allowing Him to improve upon your requests. There is something

He is an Infinite Self-Existent Spirit

powerful that happens when a child of God admits that they need God and asks Him to step in on their behalf.

It means that we cannot impress Him or put him in the position where we can do anything for Him. We cannot barter with God because we have no leverage and will never have any leverage. Many people are trying to get an angle on God. They want to find something that God wants so that they can control that and make God do what they want. God would not be in any way harmed or diminished if this world were to cease to exist or had no one respond to His invitation of fellowship and righteousness. Accept the wonder of your radical submission to God. He is God and you are not. Tell God that you realize that He is your boss. If you have tried to make foolish deals with God, admit them and repent. Ask Him what He wants you to do for Him.

We do not often contemplate how bizarre it is that God would pursue us and seek to have a relationship with us. He constantly demonstrates Himself as the God He showed Himself to be to Moses in Exodus 34 6,7.

Just stop and give Him praise that He does not gain anything by calling out to you and seeking you for redemption and yet He does it because He knows that we desperately need it.

Dear Heavenly Father,

I am amazed at the wonder of Your love for me. You know me inside and out and that I am a great sinner and yet You still pursue me. You are life itself and have been willing to reach out of the wonder of Your life in the Tri-Unity to invite and redeem me so that I can enjoy this life in You. I admit freely that I do not deserve to ever be in Your presence, but I also proclaim that as you have offered me this gift, I want so badly to dwell in Your presence and have you connect me to Your life. Take me now. I realize that I can never meet any need You have, if you actually have any needs. I cannot love You in that way because you are life itself with no needs. But I can pursue You with my whole heart and I can seek to please You. You are willing to accept these humble gifts as praise. The more I contemplate my best days, I realize how wondrous this thing called life is that You possess. I realize that I experience only a fraction of the life that You generate, but I look forward to Your remaking me here on earth and one day in heaven so that I will be able to experience the full measure of Your life.

**In the Name of the Lord Jesus Christ,
Amen**

Other verses that speak of this crucial aspect of the wonder of the Awesome God: Exodus 3:14; Deuteronomy 32:40; Job 35:6–8; Isaiah 44:6; Jeremiah 10:10; John 5:26.

No matter what you want in this life, it is nothing compared to being drawn into the presence of God. No matter how terrible life gets in this world, it is not worthy to be compared with the privilege of being invited

He is an Infinite Self-Existent Spirit

into the presence of God (Romans 8:18). God is life and our puny descriptions of life do not really compare. We are making mud pies in the gutter while He invites us into the house to eat a feast.

Cry out to the Lord to be swallowed up by His life. Cry out to the Lord to come quickly so that your life which is hid with Christ in God will finally be revealed. We wait for His Son from heaven so that our life which is hidden in Him will finally be revealed to the world but mostly to us. We await eagerly the life of God that we will be ushered into. What will it be like when God swallows us up in His life? It will be beyond what we can imagine or think.

He exists in and of Himself. He is not dependent upon any creature or thing for His existence (Acts 17:24,25). He exists by the power of His own nature (Exodus 3:14). He is the uncaused cause.

How can I take delight in the self-existence of God?

1. I can take delight in the fact that He does not need me. I can never put Him into a position where He needs me. I never have to worry that God's whole plan depends upon me. He does invite me into His plan (Ephesian 2:10). But if I fail to perform, His plan does not fail. I am free to enjoy God, follow Him, and perform all the good works that I can but not struggle with the guilt that my lack of perfection or performance somehow crippled the plan or joy of the Almighty. The main person

I hurt by not participating fully in God's plan for me is myself. God will find another way to accomplish His will if I am unwilling.

2. I can and should find delight in my dependence upon God. Just like the electric drill is completely dependent upon the power outlet for its ability to function, so I am completely dependent upon God for my life. Every time I try and disconnect from God and run my own life in my own energy, I destroy my life. I still need His energy and grace to rebel from Him. I can plug in more deeply to Jesus Christ and find life, solutions, and a relationship I did not know existed. This is called abiding in Christ in John 15. Don't just have a surface connection to the life of God. Go deep into God for He is the source of all power. Recognize that the Devil will try in various ways to get you to declare your independence from God. "Show that you can make your own decisions." Really this is "Show that you are stupid." None of us can get away from our dependence upon God. Every living thing is constantly dependent upon Him for their continued existence. God invites us as humans past a surface connection of biological life. He invites us into an eternal life – sourced and empowered by Him.

3. I can delight in the answer to the question, "Why did God create the world?" "Because He wanted to." God did not need to create the world, bugs, humans, or angels. He is completely self-contained. He created the world because He wanted to. Remember that God does not need us in any way. It is for His pleasure and His glory that

He is an Infinite Self-Existent Spirit

we exist. He chooses to love us and bless us because of the perfections of His nature and not because He has to from some deep need that arises within Him. He has no needs that we can meet. Why am I here? Because God wanted me to be here. Out of all the possible worlds that God could have brought into being, He brought this one with you and me into existence. He wanted you to exist. Delight in the fact that you were wanted – amazingly by God Himself. There were a hundred ways that He could have kept you from existing but He did not. He wanted you to exist. Embrace your destiny and give Him glory in a righteous way.

4. Take delight that God does not need our worship to somehow achieve an internal or narcissistic goal. He is not counting the minutes of worship that are offered around the world hoping that they reach some magic number. He does not need to be worshipped by anyone. The love within the Trinity is totally sufficient. It's just like when children relax when they realize that their parents love one another whether the children behave or not. God within the confines of the Trinity is being loved, stimulated, joyful, satisfied, filled with meaning and purpose. I can marvel at the Trinity – Father, Son and Holy Spirit – and see the wonder of diversity within a unity perfectly connected and fulfilled. I am safe. The world will not fall apart because the Trinity will split up. God will not suddenly expose a part of Himself to me and ask me to meet some need I was never designed to meet (Acts 17:24,25).

5. The Devil has trapped a lot of people into endless hours of religious busy work because they have mistakenly believed that God needs our service. No, He wants our love and our worship for our benefit, not His. He came to set us free, not to load us down with useless religious practices and controls. Do not get sucked into useless religiosity because some small-minded person needs to control you (Matthew 6: 1-8; Colossians 2:20-23; John 4:24).

6. Take great delight in the fact that God cannot die. It will never be true what was plastered on a major magazine cover in the 1960's: "God is Dead." This is never true even though it has been proclaimed down through the centuries by critics and atheists. All that is true is that in a few years the person who said it is dead and God is still very much alive. He is the Ever-Living One. The fact of God's containment of life itself is why the Son of God had to become a human baby. As purely God He could not die for our sins; but being born of the Virgin Mary, He could die in His humanity and pay for the death that we all should pay. His life – which cannot end – can make the trade for everyone's sins to as many as receive Him down through the centuries (John 1:12; 2 Corinthians 5:19-21).

7. The eternal question of where did it all start has an answer: GOD – a personal, infinite, self-existent spirit. This amazing being that we call God wants to have a relationship with us. He pursued us. He supplied all we need to have a relationship with Him even when we had

He is an Infinite Self-Existent Spirit

nothing to offer. Take great delight in an interactive relationship with the Supreme Being of all the beings that exist. God the Almighty wants a relationship with you. I hope you never recover from that fact. It cannot be a relationship of equals because in no area are we equal with God. But this infinite, self-existent spirit created us, planned for us, and now wants to interact with us to our joy and betterment.

The Devil wants to distract us from the incontrovertible fact that God is the only reasonable explanation for all that we have in the universe. The Devil wants you to waste large portions of your time on things that take you away from God. Satan doesn't care what you are doing as long as you are not relating to and interacting with the Almighty. We should make sure that God is interwoven through everything we do (Proverbs 3:5,6).

Chapter 4
His Attributes

In what further way may we come to know this infinite, self-existent Spirit than by studying and taking delight in His essence?

Since God is invisible we can only know Him in action. This means that our greatest working knowledge of God comes from His revealed attributes. We can look for God in these actions and operations of the universe (Isaiah 40:18; Romans 1:20).

Just as we might describe a piece of steel – to those who have never seen any – by its attributes: It is generally cold or room temperature; it is black or gray in appearance; it does not bend easily and is hard; if it is dipped in cool liquid after being in a molten state, it is brittle; it is strong; in various ways it can be shaped, molded, melted, cut; it bonds to itself powerfully even when very thin. While these do not define what steel is, they are a working understanding of some of the dominant properties and uses of steel.

In the same way the attributes of God do not define God, they give a working understanding of what He is like and how He will act. Realize that looking at God through the attributes is an objective look at a person who decides what He will do. He is not a robot who always acts in a certain way. He is defined by His essence. But we see in the attributes how He acts and displays Himself. Love is not all that God is. Love is a way that God acts in that He pursues, meets the needs, and pleases His creatures. This is how He acts. So it is consistent to say that God is loving.

Why do we make a differentiation between God's essence and His attributes?

1. When it comes to His attributes, it is no longer correct to say that God is knowledge or wisdom or power for God acts in these ways. But these do not define Him; they merely help us understand how He acts or some "property" about the Almighty. His essence is what He is and His attributes are what He does or acts like. Remember His is an infinite self-existent spirit. Do not let the Devil deceive you in a chain of false logic starting from one of His attributes. God is love. That is true, but that is not all that is true of God. The Devil can get one to embrace that God is love and then flip it around and say that love is God. This is not true. But the Devil will twist things like this and cause people to believe that anything that is not in their definition of loving cannot be from God.

2. **God makes this distinction about Himself in that He defines Himself as an infinite self-existent Spirit** (Acts 17:25,56; John 4:24; 1 Timothy 6:18; Psalm 139:7-12; Psalm 90:2). His essence relates to what He is. He does not need action or movement or context to still be God. The Devil can deceive you into falling in love with a particular attribute and to begin making that attribute your God instead of the Almighty God who acts in that way at times.

What are the attributes or qualities of this infinite self-existent Spirit we call God?

His attributes are typically divided into two types: the non-moral attributes and the moral attributes. The non-moral attributes are those attributes which have no relational or moral aspect to them. We, as humans, share very little contact with these actions and qualities that God possesses. The moral attributes are those attributes that have a relational or moral quality to them as well as the fact that we share much more contact with God in these attributes.

What are God's non-moral attributes?

Omniscience: God is all knowing and all wise

Omnipresence: God is everywhere present

Omnipotent: God has all authority and is all powerful

Immutability: God does not change

What are God's moral attributes?

Holiness: God is pure and above, beyond, and other than us.

Righteous/Just: He rewards and blesses and He punishes and exhibits wrath.

Goodness: God is loving, gracious, merciful, and longsuffering.

Truth: God is true and undeceptive.

Sovereign: God is in control.

We must remember that we have in the Bible the self-revelation of the Almighty. The attributes of God that He displays in the Bible are all that we need to know about God. But they do not exhaust the depth of the attributes that He shows us, nor do they necessarily represent all the attributes that the Almighty has or will display in the future. We would of course like to know more about this infinite, self-existent spirit; but we could not comprehend the more that we would want to know. God has explained Himself adequately in the Scriptures for us to have a clear picture of who He is and why He deserves to be worshipped as God.

God's attributes are the ways that He moves out in action. It is not proper to think of God as separated into particular attributes as though He was at one time love and another time wrath or a third time sovereign (Exodus 34:7). Every one of His attributes comes with all of the other attributes.

His Attributes

He is love but He is righteous, holy, omnipotent love not just love. He is sovereign but he is loving, merciful, omniscient, holy sovereignty. He is holiness but He is righteous, loving, omnipresent holiness.

Take delight in what you are about to learn about God and interact with Him about these powerful qualities about Him (John 17:3). We are to enjoy Him and grow in His grace and knowledge (Colossians 1:9-12)

Chapter 5
The Infinite, Self-Existent Spirit is Omniscient

What does it mean to say that God is Omniscient?

It means that He is all knowing and all wise (1 Sam. 2:3; Job 21:22; Romans 16:27)

How can God's knowledge be comprehended, defined, or understood?

Remember this is an attribute of God, not all that God is. There will be a subtle temptation to be so overwhelmed with this attribute (and each of the others also) so that we could begin to "believe" that if God knows all this, then this is all He could be or have time for. We will emphasize each attribute and in so doing potentially distort your focus on the wholeness of God to that attribute alone. It is like examining a diamond under the right lighting conditions. The diamond emits a whole array of colors and hues. It is possible to focus in on the red color to the exclusion of all the other colors. This can be helpful and instructive, but one must not lose the whole and reduce our understanding of the light from the diamond to just the red color. Remember, God is an infinite self-existent spirit and all the attributes at one and the same time.

It is helpful to focus on an attribute of God for the purpose of expanding our understanding or to give focus to our praise. We must not, however, allow one of the attributes to become our favorite to the exclusion of all the others.

His knowledge is original.

He did not receive His knowledge from another nor was He taught by anyone. Every piece of real knowledge is from God. He is the author of knowledge; it springs from Him. What He thinks is right is right. What He thinks is the best way is the best way. What He wants to do is always the most intelligent and wise. He does not have a standard outside of Himself that He must check His plans against. He is the planner and the standard which those plans must be checked against. He is the original designer and author of everything. All true knowledge comes from God or is the illumination of His knowledge (Genesis 1:1; Job 38-39; Isaiah 40:13,14; Proverbs 25:2).

His knowledge is infallible.

God does not make mistakes in what He knows. He is never corrected by some obscure fact or piece of information. He is never surprised by a discovery (Proverbs 25:2). I can remember when I was growing up our family

The Infinite, Self-Existent Spirit is Omniscient

played Scrabble. We were using a dictionary that was made before 1949. It did not have the word *radar* in it because it was not invented before the dictionary came out. A number of people think that God is constantly surprised by new inventions or new discoveries. Many people have an image of God as a tottering old grandpa in a big chair in heaven. Nothing could be further from the truth. He knows all things. He knows everything that has been invented and all things that could be invented. He also knows all things that will be invented (Job 34:21-25; Isaiah 46:10,11).

He cannot be deceived. He knows not only what was done but why it was done and the attitude in which it was done. He is supremely aware of all the conditions of knowledge. The Devil will try and smuggle into your thinking that you can hide some actions from God. You cannot hide anything from God; even the darkest night is like daylight to Him (Psalm 139:1-7; Proverbs 16:2; Proverbs 21:2).

His knowledge is instantaneous.

He has every idea, fact, and bit of information at all times immediately present to His mind. He does not need to look things up or refer to books for information. When the scientists began to discover that the whole of our universe seemed tuned for human existence, they called this the anthropic principle. It boggled the mind that over eighty-five different values were specifically tuned to allow for our existence. One scientist said that it was like a super-intelligence was monkeying with the physics. This is clearly true. God is a super-intelligence beyond our comprehension (Psalm 139:4; Psalm 147:4,5).

Objection: Does it not say in the Scripture that God went down to see the people at the Tower of Babel to see if these things were so (Genesis 11:6)?

Yes, He went down to examine but not because He did not know but in the official capacity of a judge who is about to pass judgment. Even if the judge is aware of the facts of a particular case, he must re-examine the facts in his official capacity as Judge. A parent asks the child, "What did you do?" Not because the parent doesn't know but because the parent is trying to get the child to take responsibility for the action. A parent may also ask a child to restate the events that have just transpired before they would deal out a punishment or correction to the child.

This is another expression of anthropomorphic language. God often uses human terms or idioms to explain something He is doing so that we will understand what He is doing. But God cannot be confined to this human expression or human way of seeing this event.

His knowledge is retained.

He never loses any of His knowledge or forgets what He knew. God is not able to forget nor lose track of any piece of information. He is the God of all knowledge. His mind

The Infinite, Self-Existent Spirit is Omniscient

knows and retains all knowledge (Isaiah 49:15-16; Hebrews 6:10; Psalm 50:2).

Objection: God is said to forget our sins and remove them from us as far as the east is from the west... and remember it no more (Psalm 103:12; Isaiah 43:25).

He no longer holds those sins against us because of what Christ has done on the cross as our sin sacrifice. He does not forget our sins as though that bit of information is no longer available to Him. But our new position in Christ supersedes the old position of sinner. This is much like the fact that humans cannot fly – that fact or bit of information is true. But if a human gets on an airplane, hang glider, etc., they are able to fly even though they cannot. Their new position connected to the airplane allows them to do something they cannot do in and of themselves.

"Forget" is another anthropomorphic use of language in which God is trying to help us understand what happens to the power of the sins that we have committed. If we have sinned, then we should be condemned. This should change God's relation to us. But God, being rich in mercy, does not let this change or punishment happen even though He still clearly knows all that we have done or will do. He "forgets" them in the sense that they no longer have any bearing on His dealings with us because of what Christ has done. Our position in Christ is of a new creature – a child of God (2 Corinthians 5:17; John 1:12).

His knowledge is exhaustive.

He is not eternally learning and keeping ahead of His subjects by learning as much as or at the same rate that they are. He presently knows everything there is to know. He knows what is in the darkness, the hidden things. He never learns anything.

He will never need to learn anything. He knows all about radar, computers, X-rays, and every discovery that has yet to happen. He knows all the ways to produce power. He understands every detail about miniaturization. There is absolutely nothing beyond what we know now that He does not already know (Job 38:1-4; Ezekiel 11:5; Daniel 2:20; Isaiah 40:13,14). He recognizes no lack of knowledge in future events which have as yet not occurred in time. He is as aware of past events as present and future ones (Revelations 1:8; Daniel 7:13).

He knows every possibility of every possibility.

God tells us that He is aware of what would have taken place if events had occurred differently. Example: If you were prompted by the Lord to read the Bible or pray, but you watched a TV show or read a magazine instead. God is aware of every sin and problem which will come from that decision. He is also aware of every blessing and reward that you missed because you didn't do what He prompted you to do. This means that God is instantaneously aware of all the ramifications of every decision and action (1 Samuel 23:10-13; Matthew 11:21).

The Infinite, Self-Existent Spirit is Omniscient

His knowledge is true knowledge.

He is never limited by one perspective or by one side of an issue. He equally knows a situation from the emotional, mental, spiritual, moral, and hundreds of other positions. There are many times we are in a quandary because we see that if we say what needs to be said, it will cause someone's feelings to be hurt or a relationship to be destroyed. God is never in that situation because He knows what will come from all actions and what should come from them. He knows how different people came to their particular perspectives and whether it is best to jar them out of their limited perspectives (Job 34:21-25).

How do I take delight in God being Omniscient?

1. The more true knowledge I learn, the more I am like God.

God has hidden things in the world of nature, people dynamics, and every career field that are begging for discovery. I have been asked by God to uncover this knowledge and to use it for righteous ends. God delights in our discovering the things that He has hidden in the world – whether those things are biological, geological, psychological, spiritual, or any other field of study. He wants us to discover the world as it truly is. Unfortunately the Devil is doing all he can to distort the truth so that we do not see it for what it really is. The Devil will have us miss a key truth and then pay attention to silly facts and ideas. Pay attention to the things that are true and important.

Proverbs 25:2 - *It is the glory of God to conceal a matter, but the glory of kings to search out a matter.*

The more unlearned I am, the less I am like God. I must be sure and build the foundation of my knowledge upon God for the beginning of wisdom is the fear of the Lord. Christians do not have anything to fear from true knowledge or true education. Christians down through the centuries have been champions of education and knowledge. It has only been with the advent of the myth of evolution that education has become the enemy of the Christian. If the facts about our origins are examined faithfully and not boxed in by evolutionary dogma, then the truth of God begins to shine out again. It is unfortunate that much of today's scholarship is used on excusing or explaining sin instead of uncovering the glory of God or even more tragic, trying to explain the world and our lives without God. This endeavor is "vanity of vanity" says Solomon in Ecclesiastes.

God is not a God of superstition and ignorance but a God of perfect knowledge. We must not give into the popular and growing custom of good luck charms and bizarre superstitions as though they controlled our lives. I become more like God when I learn and come to understand all the true dynamics of the world around me.

The Infinite, Self-Existent Spirit is Omniscient

2. God sees every virtuous and shameful act even those that are accomplished in secret.

God will bring to light every hidden thing and the secrets of men's heart. We may be able to hide from man but not God. God wants us to be transparent before Him -- open and honest -- especially because He already knows. (Ecclesiastes 12:14; 2 Corinthians 3:17,18). I become transformed when I admit before God that I really am both good and bad. When I try and hide some fact about myself or pretend that I am really not that way, then the Spirit of the Lord cannot come in and change me. Denial of the real issues and real story is a way to hand the Devil control of your life. If I am going to enjoy the Christian life, I must regularly, if not daily, expose myself to the penetrating gaze of God. Then I must be willing to agree with God's assessment. Take delight in the full gaze of God who knows all about us and still loves us and wants our best.

Even though no one else knows some good deed you did, God knows and will reward (Matthew 6:3,4,6,18). It is worth it to listen to the prompting of God and do something nice for your spouse, for a friend, or a co-worker. Even though no one sees, God sees and knows. When we live as though we know that God is watching, we are living by faith in the reality of God's existence. This is impressive to Him. It delights Him and us (Hebrews 11:6).

3. God is aware of every virtuous plan you conceive.

One of the startling things about God's knowledge is that He knows when you plan to do good even if you never are able to do it (Ezekiel 11:5; Psalm 139:1-3; Psalm 7:9). This is an encouragement to keep our mind clean, knowing that we will be rewarded for every attempted endeavor. While He is against scheming against others, He is for us planning to do good to others even though it may never take place because of circumstances beyond our control. Every time I plan to love another person, it is itself a good deed. Instead of allowing our minds to be filled with vengeance, selfishness, and sin, allow God to see you thinking loving, righteous, pure, and kind thoughts (Philippians 4:7,8). What good would you do for the people in your life if things were different? Think on these things and take delight in God watching your thoughts.

4. Take delight in becoming wise like God.

When I seek after God's wisdom, I am delighting in God. When I change what I would do to do what is wise, I delight God and find new levels of joy in my life. There are all kinds of decisions that you make each day and each week which if made with new levels of wisdom would change your life. God is all wise and He wants us to grow in His wisdom (the book of Proverbs). Often our fleshly nature wants us to pursue what we selfishly desire instead of what is best for everyone, including ourselves.

Almost every day I ask God how to solve the number one problem I am dealing with at that time in a wise way. I

The Infinite, Self-Existent Spirit is Omniscient

think clearly about the problem on which I need His wisdom, and I begin reading the proverb for that day. If it is the third of the month, then I will read the third chapter of the book of Proverbs. I will read slowly asking God to show me His wisdom for my specific problem. In almost every case God seems to highlight one verse out of the chapter for that day as the answer. I study that answer and think and pray through how to apply that verse to my life instead of the way I would have handled it. I am amazed at how this simple way of every day accessing God's storehouse of wisdom has changed my life.

5. **God has not made a mistake with your unchangeable features.**

People can come to believe that God shortchanged them because of a deficiency or lack of comfort or status; i.e., parentage, socio-economic level, looks, frame, temperament, lifespan, etc. God has provided in every situation ample opportunities to glorify Him and enjoy the blessings of life even when the sin of others has robbed us of what is called normal existence. Rarely, if ever, does it do any good to trace down and assign blame in these cases unless the person is a threat to harm you or others again. It is usually more profitable to cling to God and ask for His grace and power to glorify Him in spite of or in the midst of the difficulty or deficiency.

I am amazed at the number of people who want a normal life and the number of normal people who want a special life. I am not discounting the injustice of having a body that doesn't work or the evil that one person can do to another's psyche, spirit, and body. But I understand that God knows this difficulty to its depth and how to bring good out of it even if it was pure evil. Do not let the Devil win the control of your soul because you think something about your life that you cannot change is unjust. What happened to you may have been radically unjust but develop a wonderful life from this point forward with Christ's grace and your choices (Psalm139:13-15).

6. No idea, technology, or discovery surprises God.

He is aware of every combination of matter, thought, and energy that is possible. No piece of information will contradict the Christian faith. The Devil can hold some hostage by causing them to believe that they can't learn certain things lest they learn that there is no God or Christianity is wrong. This will not happen. Only a twisting of the facts or an ignoring of the facts moves towards an atheist conclusion. As one of my friends who holds two PhD's remarked, "The facts are our friends." God knows it all and when it all comes out without twisting or bias, it supports the fact that there is a God and He created the world (Ecclesiastes 1:9-10; Isaiah 42:9). We can have confidence that a true education will advance a person to become a stronger Christian. We do not have to stop learning. We do, however, need to be aware of the vain philosophies of men that try to explain our existence and meaning of our society without God. We are to be learned in righteousness but innocent in depravity.

The Infinite, Self-Existent Spirit is Omniscient

7. I don't have to heap guilt upon myself for not knowing something in the past if I didn't know it.

Of course you would have acted differently if you knew then what you know now. But if there was no way that you could know it, then let it go. God wanted it that way. God knows exactly how we will react to each situation based on the information we have. If we would have made a different choice if certain information had been available to us – unless we turned away from the information when it was presented – we are not guilty for not knowing what we had no way of knowing. Take delight in the fact that God did not get that information to you at that time. He wanted you to make the decision you made. If you ignored God's warnings or counsel, then confess, repent, and move on. If you didn't have the information, then God didn't want you to go that way. (Proverbs 1:20-22; Colossians 1:25-27)

8. God knows my future and all my possible futures.

God the Omniscient is aware of the results of every single choice I make. He has declared those possibilities of some of those choices, and I can seek this knowledge in prayer and study of Scripture and my situations. Take delight in the fact that God the Omniscient is seeking to guide you to right decisions and a better future. He knows all the options that you really have, and He will make it plain which ones to take if you will listen to Him (Acts 9: 15,16; 21:11; 27:9-31). I desire the best possible future that is the most glorifying to Him. I know that I must make choices to seize that future that He has made possible for me. I also know that He has also searched out all the possible scenarios of my life and is actively guiding me forward (Ephesians 2:10). It is important to note that the Devil wants to derail God's bright future at critical moments. He uses fear, temptation, doubt, depression, and critical comments to keep us from seeing or acting in the direction God has laid out for us.

9. He can empathize with our desire to move in a wrong direction because of our limited knowledge.

God the Omniscient has provided Himself as a High Priest who has perfect knowledge but has also experienced the pull of temptation due to a limited knowledge perspective. He has been tempted in all points like us (Hebrews 4:14-16).

A temptation is only a temptation because we do not see where it leads. All temptation is a desire to take a shortcut to blessings and pleasure. These are not truly the way to blessings and long-term pleasure, but they seem that they are. God, from His perspective of all knowing, cannot be tempted because He sees the end of every decision as clearly as we see the beginning (James 1:13).

10. His revealed knowledge is the only reliable guide in the dimensions beyond our rational categories; i.e., the supernatural.

There are many supernatural theories that have been suggested: Norse gods; leprechauns; poltergeist;

The Infinite, Self-Existent Spirit is Omniscient

reincarnation; Karma; Egyptian Book of the Dead; ascended masters; parapsychology; Satanism; etc. Each scheme about the spiritual dimensions seems to fit the supernatural realm or give a working theory of this other dimension; but they are incomplete, inaccurate, and/or dangerous when they do not adhere to God's perfect revelation about the aspects of the spiritual dimensions. God the Omniscient knows the spiritual world perfectly and completely and has told us that it is not an area where our empirical induction will work. Trust the revelation of the Bible. God gave us the truths in the Bible so that we would not be led astray by other theories or schemes on the spiritual dimensions (Leviticus 19:31; 1 Corinthians 8:4-6; 1 Corinthians 10:19,20).

Take delight in God's reliable guide to the spiritual world: the Bible. We do not have to wonder whether the practices of other religions are more helpful when encountering the spirit world. The Bible is all we need. Realize that when God wanted to help us have a clear picture of the spirit world and the afterlife, He gave us the Bible. We can follow its teaching and plan for dealing with God, angels, demons, and the spirit world.

Chapter 6
The Infinite, Self-Existent Spirit is All Wise

If Omniscience is defined as all knowing and all wise, then how is God all wise? How is that different from His being all knowing?

God is called all wise in that all of the possibilities which present themselves to His infinite mind, He always chooses that course of action which results in the best overall good and holiness. We can easily imagine a scenario in which God must choose to allow a difficult and even painful event to take place to one of His creatures so that a few hundred people can come to love Him or so that a particular event takes place that is crucial to the fulfillment of His ultimate program. Therefore it is possible to evaluate an action or a series of events as bad or harmful, from a limited perspective, while ultimately it is a good or beneficial thing. It is also possible to see that because of certain constraints (which God imposes on Himself: limited human freedom of the will; justice; cause and effect; linear time sequencing; etc.), God will allow evil, disaster, and pain so that an ultimately good outcome will arise without destroying that constraint.

It is God's wisdom that allows Him to consider all the factors that could, do, or will come to play into a decision and then to make the determination that is the best possible way to allow a situation to play itself out. Since He sees the end from the beginning and applies His infinite wisdom to the whole of our time sequence, He is not surprised or put into a no-win situation. He sees no-win situations "coming" and determines that history will not go down that road. He will, however, allow humans, civilizations, and nations to make choices that will put them into no-win situations (Deuteronomy 29:18,20; Acts 17:26,27).

In other words, the world we presently live in is not the best possible world; but it is the only possible world in which key features of humanity can be preserved. There are other possible worlds that have no crime or pain or hurt or sorrow; but they also have no choice, no justice, etc. Many people fault God's wisdom in choosing or allowing this world to exist when they can imagine other ones that are "better." But God's self-description of Himself as the All Wise God tells us that after His infinite mind examined all the possible worlds and types of existence, this world with choice, cause and effect, and, yes, even sin and rebellion is the one that will produce the overall most beneficial results. (for a further discussion of possible worlds see Alvin Plantinga's ***God, Freedom and Evil and The Nature of Necessity***). One of the beneficial results that God seems to be after in allowing the present universe to exist is creatures who in some sense freely choose to love, worship, and serve Him (John 4:23,24).

The Infinite, Self-Existent Spirit is All Wise

In what ways do we see God's wisdom?

1. In His works of creation (Proverbs 8:22-30).

It is clear that when you look at the intricate nature of the creation -- the way each species fits its environment; how all life is dependent upon one another; and the complexity and symmetry which exists at even microscopic levels -- God's choices in creation demonstrate His wisdom. When examining nature one sees incredible evidence for God's wisdom. The following are only a few of the places to detect the wisdom of God: the tilt of the earth; the speed of rotation; the ozone layer and magnetic field surrounding the earth; the teeth structures of animals; the genetic code; the systems of the human body; the nature of water; the food chain.

There are other places which display God's wisdom in creation but which would require a whole philosophy course to explore. The following are a sampling: the universal self-consciousness of man; the clear perception of other beings and objects: the imagination of man; the moral motions of man: right and wrong and its universality; the categories of the mind and its symmetry with what exists; the aesthetic impulses: the innate classification and perception of beauty and its opposite; the anthropic principle of astrophysics.

2. In the existence of real choice.

God seeks (but does not need) the worship of free beings, not robots or those coerced to love Him. Without real choice there can be no real love. God could not have made a world in which real worship and real love exist without investing that world with the capacity of choice (Genesis 3). It is true that with real choice there comes the suffering, evil, injustice, bigotry, and hatred. But it is not possible to have a world where real love exists and where real choice is absent. Of the three types of evil – natural evil, societal evil, and personal evil – all three are the result of the choices of free beings but specifically the two which we are concerned about are the result of the choice of free beings who reject God's plan and program.

3. In the Tree of the Knowledge of Good and Evil.

If God invested His creatures with real choice and then never placed anything in their path that they should not do, then He would have doomed them to rebellion against Him. Only when I can get away from some actual possibility can I exercise my free choice and come back to God who I never left. If the only choice one can make is away from God, then it will be made. So if God would have offered no opportunity to sin, then He would have been dooming Adam to rebellion. Only if there are choices that bring one back to God (even though one has never left) can one exercise true choice and not be in rebellion (Genesis 2:15-17).

4. In His works of providence (Genesis 50:20; Psalm 104:24).

God has not merely created the universe, together with

The Infinite, Self-Existent Spirit is All Wise

all its properties and powers, and is not only preserving it but He rules it (Psalm 103:19). Providence is God's ordering all issues and events for His purposes. Nothing happens without God's permission and complete understanding of its ramifications. No action or activity of anything in the universe surprises God. He has been aware of its since before He put the world into motion. He knows every place it leads and what He must do to keep it from destroying His plan and program. He even knows how to use it to accomplish His plan.

Providence is the continuous activity of God whereby He makes all events of the physical, mental, and moral realms work out for His purposes (Daniel 4:35). The evil that has been permitted to enter the world has not been allowed to thwart or destroy God's original desire. In some fashion, God's providence allows for humanity to make more righteous choices and more wicked choices and then to live with those consequences. Providence is what we now call fate, luck, chance. God is in control. In the sense that we now tend to use the words fate, luck, and chance, we are mistaken. There are no things, actions, or events that just happen. There are reasons and God ultimately is in control. This, however, should not cause us to go on a mysterious hunt to look for meaning in every leaf that falls or every improbable event. It makes a huge difference whether luck, fate, or chance are blind and undirected or whether they are directed by the hand of a wise, loving, merciful, and benevolent God. It also matters whether there is free play within the providence of God based upon individual choices and action. And there clearly seems to be in this world we inhabit. It makes a difference in my mood, my perception of opportunities, my plans, my patience, and my actions to realize that God has given our lives a range of possible destinies.

God controls a man's birth, physical structure, his lot in life. If God did not do this, then how could He have a plan for your life. Without His active involvement, you might not be equipped for His plan (Esther 4:14; Psalm 139:16; Jeremiah 1:5). God also calls individuals to work out their salvation and His plan in their lives (Philippians 2:12; Ephesians 2:10). There is some variation allowed within the plan(s) God has set out for us.

Objection: Doesn't this suggest that man does not have a free choice?

No, there is a difference between absolute freedom and real freedom within confines. Man is not absolutely free; he is truly free within the confines God draws for him. But only God is absolutely free and even He is bound by His own nature. The myth of absolute freedom is the trap of Satan promising man that he can be his own god. We are too dependent to be absolutely free and so is Satan.

God can turn the evil actions of men into blessings and benefits. He also can overrule the intent of a desired evil in that it brings a blessing or promotes His program or, at the very least, does not thwart it (Genesis 50:20; Romans 8:28). God does rule the world with a view to the happiness of His creatures. It must, however, be stated this is not His prime idea or goal. It is one of the elements that He takes into account when He allows a potential situation to actualize (Genesis 1:22; Psalm 84:11; Romans 8:28). He directly acts into His creation to change events without the whole of history being a miracle. He preserves the flow of events. Although at critical points He may redirect the flow or may act into the flow (Acts 9:3-7; 12:7). He uses natural means to accomplish His purpose: circumstances, inner restraint, reason, friends, etc. He knew the friends and other things you would need to move you at the right moment back when you were born. He arranged all this (Acts 16:26; Ezekiel 14:14).

He chooses to restrict some of His actions to only be released when people pray (James 4:2). He does other things in spite of prayers (Numbers 23:11; Acts 9:10-16). He does some things without the prayers of His people (2 Kings 19:34,35).

How can I take delight in the wisdom of God?

1. I can take delight in God's wisdom in every branch and fact of science as well as every other true discipline of learning, philosophy, history, English, music, athletics, theology, linguistics, astronomy, etc.

2. I can take delight in God that He offered the best possible world to Adam and Eve (Genesis 3) even though they did not take it. This is not the best possible world because that would have been a reality only if they had not chosen to disobey God. This world has that which is wonderful and retained part of the perfection which God gave it, and it has that which is despicable.

The choices of mankind have truly scarred and destroyed that which was beautiful, perfect, and good.

3. I can take delight in the wisdom of God in that my freedom of choice (not absolute) is a more valuable gift than a sinless world. I should use it wisely. God has given me the opportunity to love Him in a real sense. I am actually doing something significant when I choose to love God. It is significant enough for God to be willing to endure all the misery, pain, sin, rebellion, and blasphemy in the world. He has chosen to see as significant my movement in His direction (even though that movement is dependent on Him).

4. I can take delight in the wisdom of God in that my love and my choices are real and forever change reality when they are expressed. I do not live in a dream where my actions affect nothing. Every choice I make is a hinge of history. History would not be the same if I had not chosen. What I say in response to my wife, children, boss, etc., changes history. How I act today and what I do today forever changes the course of the life I live. I can turn the course of my life for the better with my small choices.

5. I can take delight in the wisdom of God that those who lived before me had choices and real consequences. I inherit circumstances and a world changed by the choices of others. My choices are limited by these prior choices, but I am not bound to no choice at all. All of the past choices affect me (pollution, defoliation, abortion, slavery, prejudice,

The Infinite, Self-Existent Spirit is All Wise

communism, unrestricted capitalism) but they don't need to define me. All of my choices, good or bad, will impact those who come after me.

6. I can take delight in the negative commands that God gives us. Every negative command God gives is a sign of His wisdom, His desire to love, His protection of His creatures, and His blessings on His children. It is as though God is giving the secrets of life hidden from others but revealed to us through the negative commands (watch out for this minefield). God does not say NO because He wants to be a big bully in the sky but because He knows the rules and make-up of the universe. He knows what to avoid. Many times the preoccupation with science fiction or certain types of novels or role-playing is a subtle form of rebelling against the universe in which God has placed you. We are called upon to live in the world as it is, not a world of make-believe. We must learn God's laws and not make a world with different ones.

I have watched a number of people get seduced into wanting to live in a Star Wars Universe or a Marvel Universe rather than the one they are in. They learn the laws and languages of these make believe worlds instead of the rules of God's Universe. God's wisdom tells us that we can know how to make relationships work; how to overcome the injustice of others; how to parent well; how to build a life of love. But for many it is too much work. They are caught by a snare of the world, the flesh, and/or the Devil and may spend their lives wanting to live in a comic-book world. How tragic that they have lost the spiritual war without even fighting.

7. I can take delight in the wisdom of God that all the philosophical (metaphysical) questions can be best answered by the biblical perspective of God, man, and the universe: the question of being; the question of knowing; the question of morals; the question of beauty; the question of form and freedom. For a beginning primer on this subject, read *He Is There and He Is Not Silent* by Francis Schaeffer.

8. I can take delight in the wisdom of God that everything that happens to me beyond my control is meant to bless me and benefit the world at large. I just need to love God in the midst of it so that the larger blessing can be birthed out of it (Romans 8:28). That which I cannot change or should not change is the best for me immediately or ultimately. I am willing to cooperate and not kick against the bars. Am I willing to discover how it is best for me (Psalm 46:10)? Every evil choice of others or even ourselves can be changed or the outcome turned by God into that which is good if we love God and seek His purpose. Our attitude really does determine our altitude. We can go as high as our ability to adjust to changing situations. God is in control. Stop whining and figure out what He is up to and how you should respond (Romans 8:28; Genesis 50:20).

9. I can take daily delight that every single day can be a treasure hunt through the wisdom of God for our lives: time schedules, activities, appointments, interruptions, impulses. Why would God put this in my schedule? Is this a divine appointment? Am I grateful for God's direction

(Ephesians 5:20)? Am I alert to God's redirection or plan or does He have to hit me over the head with a brick (Proverbs 1:22; Ephesians 5:15)?

10. I can take delight in the wisdom of God that there is only one way to come to the Father – through the Son Jesus Christ. All other plans and claims are false and deceitful (1 John 5:12; Acts 4:12). If there is one God, there is only one way to Him. Other religions which were hatched without the wisdom of God deny some crucial part or aspect of the nature of God or the plan of salvation. If God has only provided one way, are we wise enough to create other ways?

11. I can take delight in learning to appreciate the wisdom of God and not fight against it. Many times Christians are aghast at what is happening in the world as though God were the author of the horrors that man does to man. They should instead marvel at God's restraint and the gift of choice. We can also seek to perceive how God is using this phenomena and adore God for the wonder of His wisdom or rest in His wisdom. Some examples: attack on Kuwait, homosexual behavior and demands for rights, being fired, getting in an accident.

12. I can take delight that God, in some instances, waits for our prayers and even our action to redirect that flow of history. Do not give up on the big issues of our time just because they seem immovable (remember the Berlin wall). Instead, slice off small measurable amounts of the big project and pray and work towards the ultimate conclusion. We are not always fighting God if we are fighting the now of our history, culture, or nation. In fact, often we are with God to righteously oppose the flow. Do not give up on the difficult individuals God has kept in your life. Prayer, patience, and God's power can work wonders. I can really change events through honest sincere requests to Him. Amazing!!! Prayer is real and God has factored our prayers into what will and/or could happen.

13. I can take delight that God has chosen in His wisdom to share the good news of forgiveness and relations with God Almighty by humans and humans only (until right at the end of the age). God has decided to pour His message and power through frail, stubborn humans. God will get the message out through us, but it would be a shame if He were unable to use you. You'd miss out on the blessing and the reward. We have been deputized to carry a most important message

Chapter 7
The Infinite, Self-Existent Spirit is Omnipotent

What do we mean when we say God is omnipotent?

It means that God has all authority and all power (Job 9:4; Psalm 75:7; Daniel 4:35).

What is meant by God has all authority?

God has the right and the position to rule.

God is in the position of supreme authority. There is no one on an equal level with God. The Devil submits His malevolent plans to God. It is important to realize that even in His rebellion, the Devil submits to God. Yes, the Devil is plotting an overthrow of God, but he is fulfilling a job God has assigned to him since his initial rebellion (Ezekiel 28:12-19; Isaiah 14:12-14). He is the devourer of the sinful and wicked (1 Peter 5:8). The righteous angels all cry "Holy, Holy, Holy" and they are aware that God dwells on a plane and exists in a dimension that even they do not fully comprehend (Isaiah 6:1-6). In order for someone to challenge God's authority, they would have to comprehend where He is and be able to "dwell in the midst of the stones of fire." The only being other than God who has ever enjoyed that exalted position was thrown from that exalted position. Mankind is several levels of magnitude below that exalted position in which God commands all the angelic host and all the laws of the universe. Someone who would challenge God's position of authority would need to be able to handle the level of responsibility that God dispatches with ease. No other being other than God can handle the responsibility, let alone challenge the one who can. Look up these Scriptures and let yourself be overwhelmed and delighted in the supreme authority of God. (Exodus 15:8; Deuteronomy 4:39; Deuteronomy 32:8; 1 Kings 19:16; Psalm 22:28; Psalm 93:1,2; Acts 17:24).

His right to rule is established by the perfections of His being (wisdom, knowledge, love, goodness, righteousness, mercy, truth) and not by the demonstration of His sheer power nor by the acts of His will (Exodus 34:5-8). A heresy began in the Middle Ages that suggested that God ruled by His sheer unchallenged power and not because of the wisdom of inner workings of His attributes, essence, and nature. If God is in charge simply because of His power, then He could be arbitrary and cruel. But because He rules from His authority and not simply His power, we can count on the continuance of His love, grace, and righteousness.

No one else could be trusted with the authority to rule over everything in the universe. No one else could make a reasonable claim to the position of universal authority.

The Infinite, Self-Existent Spirit is Omnipotent

Everything and/or every other person in the universe is incomplete, dependent, perverted, or imperfect. God the Almighty is the only one capable of being trusted with all authority because He consistently acts for His creatures' best interest. No one else could handle the level of decisions, let alone make perfect decisions each time. God alone is capable of doing the "work" of ruling the universe. Even the significant perfections of the Devil (Ezekiel 28:12) would have encountered a meltdown if he had to handle the interactions of deity. He would like to be God, but He cannot handle it. The Devil would pervert the first decision He would make. Therefore do not let the Devil, the devourer, become a god in your life. Take delight in the fact that the Living God is God and neither you nor anyone else is God (Revelation 5:1-10).

God, in His position as Creator, created more than just the things of the universe (material, immaterial, personal, and impersonal). God also created the laws by which every part and piece of the creation as well as the individuals and groups will operate. This was all included in God's statement: "In the beginning God created the heavens and the earth." (Genesis 1:1) This creation of the infrastructure of the universe is declared in Proverbs 8:22-31).

Each of God's laws hems in those within the universe and supports His authority. It is not possible to totally rebel against God. People may rebel in how they eat but not that they eat. Do people rebel against air or gravitation? People can rebel against God's moral laws for a period of time, but they do not rebel against God's physical laws for long. Often we choose to forget about those areas in which we cannot rebel. We are like a little boy with a peashooter standing next to a castle and defiantly shooting peas against the stone walls and announcing our rebellion. God also created the consequences of every violation of His laws.

Theoretically He could have created any consequences for violating the law of gravity, but He chose a punishment that fit the crime. In every place the punishment fits the crime. We do not really see the consequences for violating physical laws as a problem. Yet we can see God as unfair when He has consequences for violating His moral law. Take delight in God's creative consequences for violating His laws. When one commits adultery, they put themselves at risk for a sexually transmitted disease. This consequence fits the punishment. Each time a society has tried to deviate from God's moral norm, it has been destroyed or collapsed internally (Rome, Southern Confederacy, South Africa, England, Sweden, United States?) from its position of preeminence and strength. God also created every power or energy which drives, moves, energizes the object of His universe. Every power has been created to only work in His creation in certain ways (Acts 17:26; Genesis 1:11,12,21).

One cannot escape from God's authority. If one seeks to violate God's authority in one area by disobeying His law, they will begin to immediately experience the consequences of that violation. Escape from God's authority is impossible (Romans 1:18).

We live under the authority of God morally, physically, and spiritually. We cannot violate His laws and then not expect to have negative consequences. In an effort to stay

The Infinite, Self-Existent Spirit is Omnipotent

balanced it is important to recognize that there are obstacles in the way of even the righteous path. Allowing adultery leads to the same consequences in every society; allowing violence to go unpunished leads to the same consequences; allowing a breakdown of respect and honor for parents and authority leads to the same consequences; allowing people to covet and believe that material goods will bring happiness leads to the same consequences in each society where it is allowed.

Nothing can take place except that God gives or has given His permission for it to take place (Matthew 10:29). Even Lucifer, the Devil, in his rebellion submits to the authority of God in everything he does (Job 1:6-12; Job 2:1-6; 1 Samuel 16:14; 1 Kings 22:19-23).

There is not a king or ruler who does not receive permission to rule by God (Romans 13:1; Proverbs 8:15; John 19:11).

God arranges circumstances and situations in which we try to accomplish something, and we are allowed to move forward while another is blocked. We have dreams planted in our minds; and then when we move to complete those dreams, this is what is called the working of providence.

Objection: How could an evil ruler receive permission to rule by a righteous God?

Because of the sinfulness of the people.

People get the ruler they deserve. The book of Judges in the Old Testament is a perfect example of the people sinning and God allowing a ruler to rise up who was as ruthless and sinful as they were. Seven times in the book of Judges, God allows His people to be ruled by a foreign nation which was ruthless so that they might learn to stop sinning against His laws.

Because of a lack of watchfulness.

At times people are not vigilant to preserve the truth or freedom that past generations have paid. They assume that as it has always been so it will always be. The Russians in 1917 fell asleep and pretended that it did not matter whether the Bolsheviks or the Czar was in power. They gave the country over to those who would destroy all the traditions and institutions of morality and religion (Romans 13:11; 1 Thessalonians 5:1-8).

In order to purify God's people.

God, at times, raises up a wicked or unrighteous ruler so that His people will be purified. In the case of the Pharaohs God allowed a Pharaoh who did not know Joseph to rise up and enslave the people of Israel. He used the time of hardship in order to purify His people and make them ready for the exodus as well as to strengthen them for the journey ahead (1 Peter 4:12,13).

In order to highlight God's mercy.

God is a merciful and forgiving God. At times people can begin to take that mercy for granted or to become

The Infinite, Self-Existent Spirit is Omnipotent

complacent with God and not realize that they need His mercy. From God's perspective the most crucial orientation is your orientation toward Him. It does and will control all other events in your life. If you allow it to get out of balance, God may need to orient you to His mercy again (Revelation 3:9; 2 Corinthians 4:7-12). The book of Exodus, chapters 8-12, detailing the exodus is an excellent example of God allowing and God acting and God preserving in the midst of an unrighteous situation.

In order to spread the gospel.

Sometimes God scatters His servants in order to get them to share their faith. Many times God's people are more comfortable with people they already know than reaching out with the love of Jesus to others who need and want the Savior (Acts 4:23-31; Acts 8:1-4).

God has decided to allow evil to accomplish His purposes. For in the perfection of His wisdom He has seen that choice is more beneficial to His creatures and His ultimate glory than no-choice robots.

One either obeys God's laws voluntarily, enjoying the benefits and the relationship with God, or one obeys God's law in rebellion, reaping the consequences (Judges 3:1-4,12; 4:1; 6:1,13).

How do I take delight in the Authority of God?

1. It means that I must obey God either to my benefit or my detriment.

It is my choice. But rebellion against God totally or ultimately is impossible. Judges, chapter 13, is the perfect example of this truth. Sampson was born to begin the process of delivering God's people Israel. He was destined to do this job for God. God even prophesied about His life and what it would accomplish. He could enjoy the fruits of this responsibility or could come to it reluctantly. Sampson surrendered to His destiny reluctantly. He did exactly what God said he would do, but he (Sampson) did not really enjoy the wonderful responsibility that God had given Him.

2. The Devil cannot ultimately win.

He lives within God's universe. He is bound by its laws. He is ultimately sustained by the one who he is rebelling against. To even continue his rebellion he must play by God's rules and boundaries. The first two chapters of Job illustrate this submission aspect of even Satan's rebellion. (Revelation 12:7-12; 20:1-3,10).

**3. We should spend our time learning the rules for the universe God has placed us in, not becoming masters of other universes; i.e., sports, games, alternate realities, science fiction, certain types of fiction, role-

The Infinite, Self-Existent Spirit is Omnipotent

playing games, daydreaming, certain types of music, certain types of dance, certain types of art, certain philosophical or sociological directions.

There is nothing wrong with these, per se, as a temporary derision or illustration or motivator; but if it becomes the whole or the dominating influence of your life, it is wrong and destructive. If you are unable or unwilling to live in God's universe under God's law, then you are spinning a dream world that is in rebellion to God's universe. This is a dangerous pursuit that is ultimately doomed to fail and to leave a number of wasted years.

4. The humiliation to which Christ submitted Himself comes into even greater relief.

He was in authority with no limits except those within the perfections of His being, and He willingly submitted Himself to all the laws and limitations that He had imposed upon His creatures (Philippians 2:5-10).

5. I should look and pray to God for reasons my life is like it is.

For it must have had to pass the bar of His authority. I must open myself to all the possibilities as to what God might be doing or want to do from here. Many times people can only open themselves to what they want God to do, and they miss or fight what God is trying to do which is a greater blessing. I must not begin the dubious process of asking God to justify His actions from my limited perspective (James 1:2-5).

6. I can trust God's authority because it is not a result of His sheer power.

If God were the ruler of my life just because He was the most powerful being in the universe, then I would be on edge in my submission to Him. It is infinitely different to submit to a being who is the ruler of the universe because of the perfections of His nature which include innumerable moral qualities. He is not a despot who wields authority with no morality. I would shrink away from a god who was just powerful and could crush the opposition. I can willingly and with all confidence submit my way to God who rules over my life by a combination of all the attributes and qualities that He reveals in Scripture (James 1:17; Exodus 34:5-8).

7. I can leave all vengeance and bitterness with God for evil done to me.

I know that no one ever really succeeds in rebelling from God's authority. I know that the person who wounded me will not get away with their offense. I also know that God is at work in that person's life just as He is in mine. While I can never say for sure, I can look for evidence of God's work in their life. I can see what they did to me as a response to what God was doing or a rebellion from what God was doing. Sometimes when I am wounded I am an innocent bystander in the way of a person's battle with God (Romans 12:19; Luke 23:34).

The Infinite, Self-Existent Spirit is Omnipotent

8. All the authority in the universe has been handed over to the Son, and He has allowed us to use that authority to accomplish the will of God.

Nothing can block the authority of God invested in the believer if he/she is operating in the will of God (Matthew 28:18 ; John 14:12,13).

What do we mean when we say that He has all power?

All power means complete and total power is available to God in every moment, in every way, and in every area (Revelation 19:6).

What are the areas of God's power?

Linguistic power: Genesis 1:3,6,9,11,14,20,24,26,28,29; Matthew 4:4; Matthew 8:18; John 6:63

Words have been called the most powerful force in the universe in that once they are spoken, they can never be recalled and they change forever those who hear them. God's words will never pass away. They have contained within themselves eternal life and preservation. It is as though His words themselves had life. The ultimate linguistic power is that your words would immediately become reality. You speak and it is. This is the kind of power that God's words contain. As soon as He speaks them, they take on that reality.

Power over nature: Psalm 107:28; Matthew 8:23-27; Luke 1:37

God has power to control natural law and to override natural law. He is above it and created it. He can speed up natural laws as Jesus did when He turned the water into wine. He can slow or reverse the natural processes as He did when He made the shadow go back up the steps or when He made the sun keep shining. The critical thing to remember is that God is not caught by the mechanism of the universe. He dwells outside of it. He has power over it and can, at times, abrogate it to accomplish His purposes.

It is important to note that when God is ready to conclude history and bring in the millennium, He will demonstrate His power through nature. The book of Revelation is full of the unleashing of the forces of nature to declare how awesome God is. God has power over nature and just as God made Job realize, we should have as much respect, reverence, and honor for the one who made the animals and the forces of nature as we have for the things themselves.

Spiritual Power: Matthew 10:28; Luke 11:20

He has the power to create a spirit (Genesis 1:1) and the power to destroy a spirit. He has ultimate spiritual power (Matthew 10:28). It is spirit power that is the more devastating force than physical power. In our age of technological destruction and accomplishment, we often believe that physical power is so awesome nothing could

The Infinite, Self-Existent Spirit is Omnipotent

be more powerful. Yet spiritual power is much more powerful. He has power over every spirit, even those in rebellion to Him.

Mental Power: Psalm 147:5

We have already seen that God knows all facts, data, and choices possible. He has all knowledge and every changing circumstance constantly available to Him. He is not overwhelmed by this torrent of information. He is never at a loss for the exact piece of information which will illuminate any situation and allow the solution to become clear. In computing language, there is no end to His computing power. One cannot even suggest a number of calculations per second which His mind can process. He has ultimate mental power.

Volitional Power: Isaiah 46:10; Daniel 4:35

God has the ultimate power of the will in that whatever He decides should take place can take place. He is never in the position in which what He wants is not possible because of an obstacle. He never has to limit His vision of the possible or reality because of a barrier. He has all the power to carry out His will. His will is supreme.

God's will is limited, but it is limited by the perfections of His nature. It is not limited by the lack of ability or power. While it is possible to say that God's will is limited, this makes it seem as though God desires to do something and yet the attributes of God hold that desire back from being realized. This is to segment God in a way that is not true. Remember, God is one. God's will never flows in a direction other than that which the perfections of His nature direct Him into. He is not a being at all conflicted internally. He is perfectly at peace in that nothing internally nor externally can attack the perfect will of God. This means that God's will always seeks to do what is perfectly wise. God's will always seeks to do that which is righteous. God's will always seeks to do that which is loving and merciful.

God can even decide that His desire will not be accomplished but that there will be a difference between His permissive will and His perfect will (2 Peter 3:9). In other words, He is not locked into the universe in such a way as to automatically transfer His perfect will into reality. He can choose to hold back His perfect will from being imposed upon reality. This verse suggests that there is a permissive will that God will allow the universe and His creatures to dwell in. It is further from the center of His will than He ultimately desires but still within the confines of His basic approval.

Emotional Power: Ephesians 3:18; Isaiah 40:28

God's emotional energy is never used up nor even diminished. He is just as capable of loving one person after having loved three million as He was the first person. We will always find the same emotional response to our same attitude. His emotions do not run low (Ephesians 3:18,19; Isaiah 40:28; Jeremiah 31:3).

The Infinite, Self-Existent Spirit is Omnipotent

God has the emotional power to control His emotions even when it is perfectly righteousness to His releasing His wrath (Romans 9:22; Numbers 14:18; Psalm 86:18). The Lord has such strength that He can contain His emotions beyond anything we can conceive. When we get to heaven and really understand how vexing human sin is, we will be astonished at the emotional power of God to put up with us as long as He did (Psalm 34:8; Revelation 22:2; Revelation 2:17; 2 Timothy 4:8; Colossians 1:8). There will come a time when patience of an almost infinite duration is no longer the quality that needs to be expressed at the proper time. God will unleash a righteous wrath upon the wickedness of mankind.

Physical Power: Job 42:2; Genesis 1:1; Nahum 1:3

God not only created all physical power – whether animate or inanimate – He retains the power over it. Just in terms of sheer physical force, God can personally – without the aid of any medium – generate more power than any force in the universe (Isaiah 40:12-27; Jeremiah 32:17).

Indirect Power: 1 Samuel 2:6

All those forms of God's power are directed through secondary agencies and conditions. These are all those miracles which are merely a speeding up of normal process or supernatural intervention of normal process or extreme coincidence of timing (John 2:7-1; 2 Samuel 6:23).

Are there things which God cannot do?

By Omnipotence we mean that God is able to do whatever He wills. His will is limited by His perfections. Therefore His power is limited to act consistently with the perfections of His being. There is no conflict in these limitations. They are really not limitations at all for He only wants to move in the direction of the perfections of His essence, attributes, and nature.

How do I take delight in God's Omnipotence?

I can take delight in God by reverencing Him with a holy fear.

By fearing God, we are referring to that form of reverence that has awe, honor, and old-fashion fear associated with it. Too often in our day we treat God as though He were just like us. We need to return to a place of huge respect, reverence, and even fear of the wonder of God. Exalt Him who is the Supreme Being in the whole universe. See the fear of God as you are already being connected to Him, and you would be afraid of disappointing Him or afraid of the consequences that He has already worked into place if you violate His will (Proverbs 1:7). Delight in the bigness, the power, the transcendence, and the authority of God.

By realizing that His power comes against anyone who is sinful (1 Peter 8:6).

The Infinite, Self-Existent Spirit is Omnipotent

We must realize that God still is against sin. While we enjoy the privilege of being sons and daughters of the King of Kings, we are still punished when we do wickedness. In Hebrews 12, God tells us that He is in fact more severe and quick to correct His children. It is a fundamental part of the fear of God to realize that now that I am in relationship with God, He is more quick to correct my sin.

I can take delight that God's power chastises those who don't believe in Him (Romans 1:18-20).

God is still in the business of bringing immediate consequences to those who violate His law. There seems to be two types of consequences that come from violating the laws of God: First, those consequences that God has built into the fabric of the universe; e.g., if you violate God's law against adultery you suffer physical problems, emotional difficulties, spiritual attack or oppression, and/or other consequences. The second type of consequences are those that God Himself arranges to come against a person. He can and does at times send a message through circumstances, problems, obstacles. It is important to say that not all of these are from God as a message.

I can take delight at the foolishness of men (and ourselves at times) for coming against God and His power (Psalm 2:4,6).

While it would be obvious that fighting the Almighty God is futile, people still do it. There are times when even we find ourselves fighting the plans and purposes of God. Stop immediately if you are constantly running into a brick wall. Re-evaluate to see if you need a new method or whether God is telling you that what you are doing is at cross-purposes to Him. We must constantly remember that we live in a fallen world in which people will fight God. They don't necessarily mean to fight God; they just want to do what they want to do. Selfishness is at the heart of sin.

I can take delight that God allows the believer to use both His authority and His power (Ephesians 1:18-23; Matthew 28:18-20).

God has given the believer the right to use His authority and power. This is an amazing fact about Christians that few take full advantage of. We live out our Christian lives in the midst of a spiritual battle, and we need the use of weapons and energy that are beyond us. God allows us to use His power to accomplish His will. Do not be timid or shy about praying that God's power would be displayed to move the work of God forward.

I can remember many times when I knew I was doing the Lord's work and something was hindering it. I would claim the authority and power of God to accomplish what God clearly wanted to do. I was sharing my faith with a man years ago, and he was clearly listening intently and ready to receive Christ. At the most crucial time, a number of garbage trucks began to make such noise that this man could not hear. We stopped and started several times and then I figured out what was happening. I prayed out loud, claiming the authority and power of Christ to do the will of God. I asked that the trucks would stop and the gospel would go out. When I finished, the trucks stopped.

The Infinite, Self-Existent Spirit is Omnipotent

I finished the presentation and the man accepted Jesus Christ as his Savior. Another time I was with a group of people visiting in the home of some folks who clearly wanted to become Christians. As we were sharing our faith, the people's birds began dive bombing us. At first it seemed cute, but then I realized that they were distracting this couple from becoming Christians. I prayed claiming the authority and power of Christ for this couple to hear the gospel. I asked that the birds not be able to fly around but be stuck on the curtain rod above the people's heads until after the gospel presentation. The birds flew down right after my prayer and then didn't move until after the people became Christians.

I can take delight in the power of God to help me overcome temptation (Romans 6:11,12).

God has given us the ability to use His power to resist temptation. Use it. Often Christians are trying to fight temptation, sin, and desire in their own power and energy. God has breathed His life into the Scriptures and made available the very power of God to say no. In fact, the world is really not interested in whether you are a better person since you became a Christian. They are interested in whether Christ has done things in and through you that they know are not possible for you.

I can take great delight in God's power insulating me against the work of the Devil (John 17:18,16).

Claim God's power to insulate you against the schemes

of the Devil just as Job did for himself and his family (Job 1). Pray that you will be protected by the power of God against the schemes that the Devil has launched against you. While it is healthy to remove or separate ourselves from sinful situations and sinful people, it is not always possible to insulate ourselves completely by our own actions. God has done something far more significant in that He has made available to us the opportunity to insulate ourselves against the corrupting influences of the world, the flesh, and the Devil.

I can take delight that God wants to empower me to share my faith in Christ. (Acts 1:8).

Be open to the prompting of God to be a witness and allow the power of God to flow through you to bring salvation to others. God will and does release His power for those situations when we are being bombarded or opposed for the sake of the gospel. We need to ask for and release ourselves to the power of God to handle situations that are beyond us. We can regularly find ourselves saying things that amaze others and even ourselves. God just seems to take over and put words in your mouth.

I can take delight in using the power of God to throw mountains out of the way of God's will in my life (Matthew 21:21,22).

I have watched God do incredible things to free up a path to accomplish God's will. I have watched him move

The Infinite, Self-Existent Spirit is Omnipotent

strangers to give thousands of dollars for a new building. I have watched people suddenly move out of a town because they were in the way of God's will in their church. I have watched people be healed so they could accomplish the will of God in their job. I have watched people die as they stood against what God was clearly doing. I have watched people be delivered from demonic spirits and for the first time in years be able to choose what is right and be free from the voices. I have watched new jobs open up when they were not available so people could stay and work in a ministry. I take great delight in God's power being shown and the will of God going forward. I am greatly comforted that the God I serve is the one who holds all power. We don't have to hope for cleverness or worldly power; we serve the powerful Living God.

I can take great delight in the fact that I know who wins in the end. Every knee will eventually bow before the Lord Jesus Christ (Philippians 2:10).

One day it will be obvious that God is the most powerful being in the universe. At times it now seems that Christians are in the minority. But one day we will be recognized as those who were and are on the right side. God will display His power and majesty to everyone. He will make every knee bow. Some will do it under much duress. Some will do it with great delight. But all will do it. You serve the Living God who has chosen to give people a real choice as to whether to have faith in Him or not. Those who don't trust Him will have the ultimate shock at death.

Chapter 8
The Infinite, Self-Existent Spirit is Omnipresent

We have said that since God is invisible, the only way to "see" Him is to watch Him in His attributes, actions, and names. We are presently exploring His attributes. His attributes may be divided into two categories: the non-moral attributes and the moral attributes. We have already looked at the first two of His non-moral attributes: Omniscience and Omnipotence. The third of His attributes is OMNIPRESENCE

The Omnipresence of God is His Immensity in relationship to His creatures

Let God tell us in the Scriptures of His omnipresence:

Psalm 139:7-12 - *Where can I go from Your Spirit? Or where can I flee from Your presence? If I ascend to heaven, You are there; If I make my bed in Sheol, behold, You are there. If I take the wings of the dawn, If I dwell in the remotest part of the sea, Even there Your hand will lead me, And Your right hand will lay hold of me. If I say, "Surely the darkness will overwhelm me, And the light around me will be night," Even the darkness is not dark to You, And the night is as bright as the day. Darkness and light are alike to You.*

Presence means close, near, at hand and Omni means all or everywhere. He is always at hand or near to us. He is outside our universe but nearer to us than if He were right next to us. Whatever dimensions that He dwells in that are beyond the 10+ dimensions of our own universe, they place Him immeasurably near to us. We can picture it like it is done in the book, *Flatland*. All the people are two-dimensional beings and God is pictured as a three-dimensional being. Because He dwells in a third dimension beyond the two dimensions of the people in the book, God can be closer to each person than any person is to any other person in the two-dimensional space. He hovers over and around the two-dimensional space in this illustration of how God hovers in and around us because He dwells in an infinite dimensional place that is His alone.

His immensity points to the fact that God transcends all space and is not subject to its limitations. Since we perceive things spatially, it is difficult not to perceive everything -- including God -- spatially. God, however, tells us things about Himself that cannot be understood within a spatial context. God is not localized but instead is a spirit being that is everywhere present. God is a unique spirit in His omnipresence. Other spirits can be localized even though they seem to move quickly.

God is not everywhere present in that He is so big that all of Him covers everywhere, but rather He is everywhere present with all that He is. This concept cannot be grasped by imagining God as a huge person or being. It is more accurate to conceive of Him in these terms like radio waves. Everywhere they are present, they contain the whole

The Infinite, Self-Existent Spirit is Omnipresent

message or radio show. God is everywhere present with all that He is (Psalm 139:7-12; Jeremiah 23:24,25; Amos 9:2).

God is "close" (immanent) – to every part of His creation. God is everywhere. There is no thing that is outside of where He is. It is impossible to get beyond God for there is no "place" beyond Him. God is in a certain sense our environment. As the sea is for the fish or the air for the bird; so for everything in the universe, God is the medium in which it moves. The universe springs from that which is spiritual and operates because of His person in His person (Acts 17:28). God chooses to allow our limited dimensional universe to exist within His eternity. When we step out of this world at death, we enter His reality. It is His reality that is the true reality and ours that is a bubble of limitation within the eternity of God.

OBJECTION: This sounds like pantheism (everything is God) where God is in everything or the sum total of all that there is.

No, there is always a distinction between God and His creation. He is separate from His creation. The creation is not the pieces of God. What is being said here is that no part of God's creation is farther from God than any other part of His creation.

OBJECTION: The Scripture says that God comes to dwell in us. If He is already there by being present everywhere, how does He come to dwell in us?

This represents an equivocation of terms: God is clearly not present in the same sense of the word present in every place.

During the Old Testament He has localized some aspect of Himself in the temple. Even in the act of dedicating the temple, Solomon – and later Isaiah – realized that God's localized presence did not negate God's transcendence and omnipresence (1 Kings 8:27; Isaiah 66:1). We see a number of examples of the presence of God being "stronger" or different in one person or in one circumstance over another (Revelations 3:20; 1 Corinthians 6:19).

Let's take a look at another common fallacy involving God's omnipresence. Some have said that when a person is damned to hell, they are away from the presence of the Lord forever. But that is not technically correct because it is not possible to be "away" from the presence of the Lord completely. Hell is clearly not a separation entirely from the presence of God. In fact, it is the unrelenting presence of God in wrath that makes hell, hell. Hell is, however, devoid of God's presence in one sense – in His grace, longsuffering, and joy. Those who have chosen to embrace their selfish and ultimately sinful promptings will bear the penalty of their error just as the angels will. They will be removed from the gracious presence of the Lord and only see the righteousness and justice of God containing evil (Psalm 139:7-12; 2 Thessalonians 1:9).

God's omnipresence is in proportion with the reaction of the person to God's grace and call. God is available to everyone, but what we perceive of God is determined by

The Infinite, Self-Existent Spirit is Omnipresent

our pursuit of Him. This explains why so many people miss God – because their own heart is twisted or evil. Look at what the Scripture says in multiple places about why many miss God entirely.

2 Samuel 22:26,27 - *With the kind You show Yourself kind, With the blameless You show Yourself blameless; With the pure You show Yourself pure, And with the perverted You show Yourself astute.*

God is not immanent or present to the dog in the same way He is to the man or to the angel. We must learn to perceive God's presence. God is not present to the wicked in the same way that He is present to the righteous. We perceive God according to our basic inner attitude. It is no wonder that those who are immoral or wicked perceive God as evil or cruel (Psalm 18:26; Matthew 5:8). Since God is a unity or indivisible in His omnipresence, He is everywhere present with the whole of His being (Deuteronomy 6:4). A piece of God is not stationed in one particular place. We do not have to wonder which part of God we are addressing or which part of God is near to us. All of God is near to us.

God is omnipresent or immense in a way different than just saying that He is big. His omnipresence should not be understood in spatial terms. He is not limited by our natural laws but can be everywhere at the same time without hurrying from place to place. This, however, is not true of the Devil who is fast but localized. He needs demons to carry out his work (Ephesians 6:12). God exists on a different plane of existence than we can even comprehend. Our greatest mistake when thinking of God is to imagine Him as only a larger version of ourselves. He is above, beyond, before, over, and completely transcends everything we are or could become (Isaiah 40:18).

How do I take delight in the Omnipresence of God?

1. I can be assured that God is near to me and all His wisdom is there also.

No matter where I go there is no God forsaken place. In fact, in the place of solitude and barrenness I can often focus better on perceiving God. But He is in every place in the same way. It is my inability to pick up the incoming messages and presence of God – that is the problem (Psalm 139:7-12). There is no city, divorce, battle, or church in which He is not present. He is there and He has a way He wants you to act, speak, and emote in order to make the most of that situation. Most of the times we are trying to invent what we want to do in various situations and relationships and hoping for a good outcome. Don't guess what to do. Listen for His voice. Act wisely and watch your life change. There are better ways to play the game of life. God's ways. Sometimes in some situations the right thing to do is to leave because all the options are wicked. We are often too enamored with our own plan. We must be willing to find God in the midst of every situation (Proverbs 1).

The Infinite, Self-Existent Spirit is Omnipresent

2. I can delight in God's omnipresence that my prayers do not have to go a great distance, but they only have to escape my lips and He hears them.

God is in the extra dimensionality of eternity and is right next to me at all times. He truly is around me. My prayers don't have to travel to the outer reaches of the galaxy but only have to be formed in my mind, and He who is everywhere hears them. When we talk with God, we are talking to the one who is right next to us in dimensions that are above, over, and beyond ours (Matthew 6:1-12; Jeremiah 23:24).

3. Since God is present even when I am facing temptation, He is there to show me the way of escape.

God has told us that there is no temptation or test that can come to us that He has not provided a way of escape. But it is better than that. Because we now know that God is everywhere present, we know that God hasn't just made sure that there is a path that leads away from the temptation. We know that He is there in that moment of temptation. We can appeal to Him to make sure that we see this escape route. Just because I do not perceive the escape or do not want it does not mean that it is not there (1 Corinthians 10:13).

4. God is engaged and not just watching everything that is happening.

At times He chooses to do nothing and other times He chooses to become an active participant in a specific event. God is not just a casual observer. He is the sustainer and involved God. God is not bound by the science fiction directions of the movies or television of noninterference. Prayer is one of our ways of activating His involvement (Psalm 139:13-16; Jeremiah 29:10-14). One of the most famous verses in the whole of the Scriptures comes out of a sense of frustration that people had with God. They were accusing Him of not seeing or not caring about their plight. He responded by saying that the people did not know how to wait on the Lord. The problem was not on God's end but on the people's end.

Isaiah 40:27-31 - *Why do you say, O Jacob, and assert, O Israel, "My way is hidden from the Lord, And the justice due me escapes the notice of my God"? Do you not know? Have you not heard? The Everlasting God, the Lord, the Creator of the ends of the earth does not become weary or tired. His understanding is inscrutable. He gives strength to the weary, And to him who lacks might He increases power. Though youths grow weary and tired, And vigorous young men stumble badly, Yet those who wait for the Lord will gain new strength; They will mount up with wings like eagles, They will run and not get tired, They will walk and not become weary.*

5. I must develop eyes to perceive God – for He is there.

The prophets Isaiah, Jeremiah, and Amos proclaim that God is all around; but His people don't want to see Him. They were afraid of the changes that He would make if they were to acknowledge Him. In the New Testament, Jesus quotes these prophets in regards to many of the religious people that He encounters.

The Infinite, Self-Existent Spirit is Omnipresent

Matthew 13:14-15 - ...*And in their case the prophecy of Isaiah is being fulfilled, which says,* "You WILL KEEP ON HEARING, BUT WILL NOT UNDERSTAND; AND YOU WILL KEEP ON SEEING, BUT WILL NOT PERCEIVE; FOR THE HEART OF THIS PEOPLE HAS BECOME DULL, AND WITH THEIR EARS THEY SCARCELY HEAR, AND THEY HAVE CLOSED THEIR EYE'S LEST THEY SHOULD SEE WITH THEIR EYES, AND HEAR WITH THEIR EARS, AND UNDERSTAND WITH THEIR HEART AND RETURN, AND I SHOULD HEAL THEM."

If I can perceive "where" God is moving in strength and what He is doing, I can then work with Him more harmoniously.

John 5:19-20 - *Jesus therefore answered and was saying to them, "Truly, truly, I say to you, the Son can do nothing of Himself, unless it is something He sees the Father doing; for whatever the Father does, these things the Son also does in like matter. For the Father loves the Son, and shows Him all things that He Himself is doing; and greater works than these will He show Him, that you may marvel."*

This is essential if I am to work the works of God, and if I am to rid myself of an egocentric view of the world. God is not necessarily interested in what you think about a situation or idea. He is very interested that you discover what He thinks and what He is going to do and what He would like to do through you.

6. My relationship with God does not have to end as I move from activity to activity or situation to situation.

I am not closer to God at church than doing something else. I may be more pleasing to Him doing certain things, but I am not closer to Him. I may feel more in harmony with God and His purposes, but the distance is the same. I am not closer to Him at church than at work. I do not move away from Him when I am on vacation or at the golf course or sleeping or driving the freeways. I can pursue Him in any situation and at any locale. In fact, my spirituality really depends on my ability to find and pursue God in any and every situation and location. At whatever point I stop pursuing Him, it is at that point that I am no longer connecting with the person who is present everywhere.

Chapter 9
The Infinite, Self-existent Spirit is Immutable

What do we mean when we call God immutable?

We mean that God is unchanging in His essence, attributes, purposes, and promises. He is exalted above all causes. He is the ultimate cause and frame for all actions. This does not, however, mean that God is static or will not react to a change in His creatures. His nature does allow for variation within a fixed form. This is the age-old form and freedom problem. He is the form and He allows for the freedom without destroying the form. Without the perfections of God's being, there is no answer to the form and freedom problem. Look at what the Scripture tells us. This is the raw material for our understanding and definition of immutability. Whatever we may want immutability to mean, it is the Scriptures that define what it actually means.

Numbers 23:19 - *God is not a man, that He should lie, nor a son of man, that He should change His mind. Does He speak and then not act? Does He promise and not fulfill?*

1 Samuel 15:29 - *He who is the Glory of Israel does not lie or change His mind; for He is not a man, that He should change His mind.*

All change is either for the better or the worse and since God cannot get better, any change in Him would be for the worse. Since this is not possible, He clearly cannot change. Look at the following Scriptures to begin helping you understand and take delight in God the infinite, self-existent spirit who is immutable. Do not skip reading these verses.

Malachi 3:6 - *I am the Lord, I change not.*

James 1:17 - *All good and perfect gifts come down from the Father of Lights with whom there is no variation or shadow caused by turning.*

Hebrews 13:8 - *Jesus Christ is the same Yesterday, Today and Forever.*

Psalm 102:25-27 - *In the beginning you laid the foundations of the earth, and the heavens are the work of your hands. They will perish, but you remain; they will all wear out like a garment. Like clothing you will change them and they will be discarded. But you remain the same, and your years will never end.*

Psalm 33:11 - *But the plans of the Lord stand firm forever, the purposes of his heart through all generations.*

Psalm 110:4 - *The Lord has sworn and will not change His mind.*

Proverbs 19:21 - *Many are the plans in a man's heart, But the counsel of the Lord it will stand.*

Isaiah 46: 10 - *I make known the end from the beginning, from ancient times, what is still to come. I say: My purpose will stand, and I will do all that I please.*

The Infinite, Self-Existent Spirit is Immutable

1 Corinthians 1:20 - *For no matter how many promises God has made, they are "Yes" in Christ and so through Him the "Amen" is spoken by us to the glory of God.*

Hebrews 6:17,18 - *In the same way God, desiring even more to show to the heirs of the promise the unchangeableness of His purpose, interposed with an oath, so that by two unchangeable things, in which it is impossible for God to lie, we who have taken refuge would have strong encouragement to take hold of the hope set before us.*

It is very important to examine each of the above areas to determine exactly what immutability does mean. Many people have extended immutability past its meaning and begun to define God using logical and philosophical categories that are not biblical. It is very easy to take some of the Scriptural data and build a God who is static and unmoving. This can be a deception by the Enemy to diminish your faith because you logically have not understood who God is and who He is not. Remember that the Living God dwells in a dimensionality many levels beyond our own. He is dynamic and brilliant beyond all knowing. The Devil wants us to believe that God is static, a traditionalist, an unfeeling and not modern being. But that is not what immutable means. Immutability means there is nothing about His essence that can decay, progress, or be different. His essential being will always be what it is. He will always have the same value for love, goodness, compassion, and gentleness. He will always see gain at others' expense as wrong, no matter how popular it is in a culture or time period. He is life itself but He does not evolve. We can decay, progress, and be essentially different.

Take great delight that what is good will always be good. You will not live your life according to one standard but then find when you are in heaven God has "grown" or "changed" where what you thought was good is now bad. His definitions of love, mercy, righteousness, and holiness will not change. You can rest in His unchanging grace.

He does react. He does feel. He does adjust His plans because of the choices of His creatures. He does not diminish. He does not change His morals. What was righteous is still righteous. The basic underpinnings of a moral society will always emanate from God: You shall not do harm to others. You shall not gain at the expense of others. You shall be wise (finding the triple win – where God is glorified, others win, and you win). The wicked can and should lose because they spread loss to others so they can gain.

Recently our society has begun to change its moral boundaries. Not because the things that were wrong before no longer cause harm but because the gain that certain individuals want and the society wants are the great prize, and we have made people forget about the harm that is done by changing the moral boundary lines. We no longer want to hear about the harm our new morals are causing. This always results in the destruction of that culture, nation, or people. Let me give you a quick list of the new morality that is really harming others; we just don't want to know about it: women's rights through killing our unborn; any form of sexual expression is okay if you feel something; millions of dollars being stolen through clever advertising in a gambling scheme; verbal

The Infinite, Self-Existent Spirit is Immutable

abuse is now free speech; overworking and underpaying employees to gain more profit; stealing from companies because they won't miss it; scheming to take others' goods is now called sophisticated business investing.

OBJECTION: Did not the second member of the Trinity take on humanity when He became incarnate? Does this not suggest a change in the essence of God?

The answer to this is NO!!!

Christ did not change in relation to His deity through the addition of His humanity. Let's explore a little history in order to answer this question. The early church spent considerable time discussing this question and ones like it (centuries in fact). The great debate about the nature of Christ and whether Jesus can really be God if He is in any sense human rocked the church throughout the fourth and fifth centuries. A group sprang up in the church calling themselves Arians saying that Jesus was some form of a lesser God because He was human (much like the Jehovah Witnesses of our day). They gained quite a following and the question of how Christ can be fully God if He is also human needed to be decided.

In 325 AD at the Council of Nicea the church adopted this creed to explain the nature of the Son of God:

"We believe in one God, the Father Almighty, Maker of all things visible and invisible. And in one Lord Jesus Christ, the Son of God, begotten of the Father (the only begotten; i.e. of the essence of the Father), God of God, and Light of Light, Very God of Very God, begotten, not made, being of one substance with the Father; by whom all things were made (in heaven and on earth); who for us men, and for our salvation, came down and was incarnate and was made man; he suffered, and the third day he rose again, ascended into heaven; from thence he cometh to judge the quick and the dead. And in the Holy Ghost. And those who say; there was a time when he was not; and he was not before he was made; and he was made out of nothing, or out of another substance or thing, or the Son of God is created, or changeable, or alterable; they are condemned by the holy catholic and apostolic church."

This was not clear enough for some and after almost 125 years of continual wrangling on how to understand the nature of the Son of God, the church came together in 451 AD and produced the Chalcedonian creed at the Council of Chalcedon:

"Following the Holy Fathers, we unanimously teach one and the same Son, our Lord Jesus Christ, complete as to his Godhead, and complete as to His manhood; truly God, and truly man, of a reasonable soul and human flesh subsisting; consubstantial with the Father as to His God head, and consubstantial also with us as to His manhood; like unto us in all things yet without sin; as to His Godhead begotten of the Father before all worlds, but as to His manhood, in these last days born, for us men and for our salvation, of the Virgin Mary, the mother of God; one and the same Christ, Son, Lord, Only begotten, known in two natures, without confusion, without conversion, without severance, and without division; the distinction of the natures being in no way abolished by their union, but the peculiarity of each nature being maintained, and both concurring in one person and hypostasis. We confess not a

The Infinite, Self-Existent Spirit is Immutable

Son divided and sundered into two persons, but one and the same Son, and Only-begotten, and God-Logos, our Lord Jesus Christ, even as the prophets had before proclaimed concerning Him, and He Himself hath taught us, and the symbol of the fathers hath handed down to us."

The early church answered the question, therefore, that to add humanity to the second member of the Trinity did not in any way change or affect the essence of God. There was no convergence or confusion. God is immutable but not static.

Take delight in this aspect of God as He explained Himself to us by sending the Son of God as the perfect expression of Himself. It did not change the essential nature and being of God to become human through the incarnation of Jesus the Christ born of the Virgin Mary. We could not have seen nor expected this unique revelation of the person of God. It shows us that while God is immutable, He is dynamic and not static. God brings out of His immutable self that which we could not expect but which benefits us, teaches us, delights us, and overwhelms us. What does God have in store for those who love Him?

Psalm 103:17 - *But from everlasting to everlasting the Lord's love is with those who fear him, and his righteousness with their children's children.*

Genesis 18:28 - *Far be it from you to do such a thing - to kill the righteous with the wicked, treating the righteous and wicked alike. Far be it from you! Will not the judge of all the earth do right?*

OBJECTION: Doesn't the Scripture say that Jesus laid aside His deity in Philippians 2:5-10? Doesn't this suggest a change in the attributes of God?

The answer is NO!!!

Let us look at Philippians 2:5-10 in more detail. This section of Scripture says that He laid aside the independent use of His attributes and submitted Himself to the other members of the Trinity, so He might be able to purchase our salvation and so that He could be a true example of the Spirit-filled life. If Jesus had relied upon His deity to accomplish the life He lived, then He would not have been an example for us. What He did was dependent upon the other members of the Trinity even though He could have done it all out of His own divinity. Having completed His mission, He again exercises full independent use of His attributes.

OBJECTION: Doesn't His plan seem to change at times?

Don't His purposes seem to be thwarted?

Don't His promises seem to be fading like cut flowers at times?

Yes, in fact some of the most direct challenges to God as Almighty come from this area.

OBJECTION: There are a number of places in Scripture that God is said to have relented or changed His mind (Genesis 6:6; Exodus 32:14). How do we understand this in light of His immutability?

The Infinite, Self-Existent Spirit is Immutable

God told Moses of His desire to destroy the people of Israel because of their idolatry, stubbornness, rebelliousness, and wicked ways. Moses appealed to God on the basis of three things: These were His people, the Egyptians would see God as evil for bringing these people out to kill them, and God had made a covenant with Abraham, Isaac, and Jacob. The Scripture says that because of Moses' prayer and humility, God then changed His mind. God pivoted His will to allow for the change in Moses' heart. Interestingly enough, all the people except Moses, Joshua, and Caleb perished in the wilderness as God had said He would do. Moses bore the burden of leading the people God wanted to destroy, and he lost the ability to go into the Promise Land because of dealing with them.

What are the possible solutions to this apparent contradiction to God's immutability?

1. God only said He would destroy His people in order to move Moses into expressing more identification with the people, so he would not give up on the people later when he would be so tempted. In other words, God needed to intend on destroying the people to get Moses to really become their leader. God would have destroyed the people if Moses had not intervened, but that was not God's purpose. His purpose was to bring Moses to a deeper identification with the people for the long road ahead. God's plan, therefore, was accomplished.

This type of example is illustrated in the Tower of Babel

where the purpose of God was not to confuse the languages but to disperse the people – which took place.

A note of application. Many times what God seems to be doing is only the means to a greater or completely different end. Don't refuse to look to the end result of God's dealings and trust Him.

2. This instance shows the range of God's will. There is His perfect will and His permissive will. In this way God allows for free choice. This is supported by 2 Peter 3:9 and by the real call to change before the flood as well as Jesus' announcement, "Repent for the Kingdom of Heaven is at hand."

In this case God really wanted to destroy His people as the best of the best solution, but Moses' request moved God to allow His permissive will carrying out His perfect will. The same takes place in the case of Hezekiah and the opposite in the case of Nebecanezzer and his insanity.

A note of application. If we come to understand God's perfect will in a particular area, we are foolish to seek to change it through prayer or direct action just because it is painful. We seem to be allowed to follow a lesser version of His will. He has not created us as robots who must do what He says. In some way we are involved in the obedience and the disobedience.

3. Moses is the representative of the people and because of his change in relation to God, God could change in relation to His people. This is clearly the case in Nineveh with Jonah and King Saul and his loss of the Kingdom. The truth of representation is clear in Adam's sin and in Levi paying taxes through Abraham. Those who are the official representatives of a people hold the fate of many people in their hand.

A note of application. This is clearly the case when the leaders of the United States outlawed prayer in public schools. They, as the representatives of the nation, declared that they did not want God protecting the nation. A titanic shift has taken place in the education and morals of the nation since that time. We have been on a downhill slide morally since that decision. God takes what the leaders of a people say very seriously. Do not take lightly your position as a leader if you are put into such a position. It affects far more than just yourself.

Jeremiah 18:7,8 - *If at any time I announce that a nation or kingdom is to be uprooted, torn down and destroyed, and if that nation I warned repents of its evil, then I will relent and not inflict on it the disaster I had. And if at another time I announce that a nation or kingdom is to be built up and planted, and if it does evil in my sight and does not obey me, then I will reconsider the good I had intended to do for it.*

4. This is anthropomorphic speech about God in that God's real relation to our choice and His will is just incomprehensible to our understanding, so He has accommodated His actions to our understanding and

mental ability. He didn't really change His mind; it just looked that way to us.

This was illustrated in Christ's dwelling here on earth. It looked like God was divided while Christ lived on earth, but the relation between the members of the Godhead is beyond our ability to comprehend. Their connection remained on a plane that we are unable to penetrate. God the Father, God the Son, and God the Holy Spirit were and are still One even though one can see interaction and perhaps physical distance between them.

5. God's intent was to spare His people, but His justice demanded that He destroy them unless something changed around which His mercy could come into action. In other words, God wanted Moses' participation and planned on receiving it.

A note of application. God often will withhold action because we are uninvolved either in prayer or action; e.g., Eli and his sons. This seems to be the way in which prayer often works when it comes prompted from the heart and will of God. He desires to act and limits Himself to responding to our prayer.

In 2 Samuel 24:16, God acted differently because of David's actions. David's actions of repentance and prayer brought to the forefront a different attribute of God's nature than his sin did. God Himself tells us how to handle many of these passages which deal with God doing something different than at first He declared He would do. This difference involves the reality of a true free choice.

The Infinite, Self-Existent Spirit is Immutable

A note of application. We must come to terms with the fact that God exists and moves by the perfections of His nature, not the sheer effort of His naked will. This means that His attributes will respond differently to different situations. It also means that God at times can be suggested to be caught by the perfections of a particular attribute until something changes so that another perfect attribute can be displayed. We must learn to respond to the prompts of God and be the pivot around which a particular attribute can be displayed.

How do I take delight in the Immutability of God?

Hebrews 13:8 - *Jesus Christ is the same yesterday and today, yes and forever.*

We can be assured that the same God that Moses, Elijah, and Abraham prayed to is also our God.

God has not grown or changed. We are not dealing with a more evolved God than the ancients did. The truths of God and the reactions of God will be entirely consistent with who He is revealed to be in the Bible. Jesus in arguing with the religious leaders of His day – who did not believe in the resurrection or life after death – pointed out that God declares after Abraham, Isaac, and Jacob had died, "I am the God of Abraham, Isaac, and Jacob."

God worked with these men and women of faith, and He will work with us. The same ways that He moved in their life, He will move in ours. The Bible is relevant precisely because God is immutable. If God changed, then we would need a new Bible to understand this "new" God. But thankfully He is the same yesterday, today, and forever.

Take delight that God is still doing miracles.

There is a subtle tendency to read the stories of how God has worked in the past and to believe that God doesn't work that way in the present. But it is the same God, and He still does miracles in our day. The danger is that if we do not see a miracle happen, we tend to not believe that it happened. Many of the people who were alive when the Bible was written did not see the miracles either. God is at work in the world today. We may not see as much of His work as we can read about in the Bible. But we should not deny that it is possible or that it is happening.

Take great delight that God — who specializes in working with nobodies — is the God who chose you.

God has specialized in taking nobodies that the world has discarded and making them useful and powerful for Him. Abraham was a nobody and yet God used him. He

The Infinite, Self-Existent Spirit is Immutable

was one of only a few who had true faith in that time, and yet God used that little beginning to bring salvation to the whole world. Moses was discarded by the world as a murderer. He was too old having spent his "useful" years in the wilderness of Midian. Gideon was too scared to really amount to much for God. Yet God met his fear at each stage and energized him so that he became a mighty warrior for God. God took a sheepherder and fig picker named Amos and commissioned him to speak to the king about sin and corruption. We still feel the power of Amos' message.

Take delight and comfort in the fact that God still hates the same sins that He did in the Bible.

Find great joy in the fact that good is still good and evil is still evil. It is still morally praiseworthy to help someone. It is still wrong to gain at another's loss. This will always be the case because God will always sit on the throne. One of the regular insults hurled at Christians is that they have not kept up with the modem times. Nobody believes that adultery is wrong anymore. Nobody believes that coveting is bad. Only weird people refuse to respect the other religions of the world. Yet God is unchanging. What He said was wrong thousands of years ago, He still feels is wrong today. What is wrong is still wrong because it still does harm to people when it is done. What is good is still good because it benefits all those in the society, not just a few. It is always helpful and enlightening to read the Bible for the righteous standards that emanate from God's immutable person. God is clear about what pleases Him and what does not. It is a crucial error if we begin to think that God has changed His mind because we are living thousands of years after the time of Christ.

Take delight in God for the wonder of His unchanging dynamic perfection of being.

We can stop and stare in awe that God never runs down. He never needs to go in for repairs or tune-ups. He doesn't need million-year check-ups. He is perfection. God has never changed the perfections of His nature nor needed to grow or adjust to any new situation. It is amazing to contemplate the wonders of God over time. We live in a world in which everything runs down. Everything decays and becomes more disorganized. We can praise God that somehow in the internal makeup of who He is that He never shifts, changes, decays, grows, or develops. He is always the same without any laws of decay affecting Him. There will not come a time billions of years from now when God will be different or diminish in some way. He will always be what He always has been.

The Infinite, Self-Existent Spirit is Immutable

Take delight that God will prompt us to change our churches and the ways we worship Him to help the next generation see the wonders of His unchanging grace and being.

God is regularly updating our perception and experience of Him. The world needs to see all the wonders of Him. We are the conduit that God pours His grace through. He will move upon our hearts the way a guitar plays the same six strings and yet gives a totally different melody. God moves upon our heart and shows us what has been there all along. We need to realize that if we hang on to any one perception of God too long or too tightly, we can and may move to heresy. God will highlight who He is in different ways at different times. Our growth is an ever-widening appreciation of the wonder of God. This year He might show you His power, next year His mercy, the year after that His knowledge. Let God show you Himself in the way that He knows that you need to see.

Take delight in the fact that the unchanging, infinite self-existent spirit will accomplish His purposes.

It is exciting to realize that we are on the winning side. The Bible concludes essentially with: Jesus wins. It is possible to get down and struggle because the world, the Devil, and the flesh seem to be winning all the adherents. Christians can, at times, seem like a desperately small minority. But God is unchanging; He is in charge and He will be in charge. The unchanging One who holds the universe together has told us how things turn out. He is looking for people who will worship Him in spirit and truth (John 4:24). You are not foolish to align your fate with the unchanging God of the universe.

Chapter 10
His Attributes:
He is Holy

We begin to examine the most significant statement about God that could possibly be made—He is HOLY!

An attribute is a way of describing one aspect of God. Each attribute looks at a particular way God acts or the way He describes himself. An attribute of God is not a segment of God but a way that He is. In other words, within God's knowledge He is omnipotent, loving, merciful, just, and so on. Within God's holiness He is loving, sovereign, immutable, righteous, and so on. This idea of each attribute controlling or affecting every other attribute is the most important element about this attribute of holiness.

What do we mean when we say that God has moral attributes?

The moral attributes are those attributes that have a relational or moral quality to them. As humans, we share much more contact with God in these attributes, meaning that there are certain aspects of God we are able to understand in a moral way. In other words, we can attach the quality of "good" or "bad" to them. We can, in a sense, "judge" God for in His actions these parts of His being are exposed. But when we say we can "judge" God, it is the perfections of His nature that are the definition of what is moral, so we only understand what morality really is by how God acts. Some have attempted to pit one particular action of God mentioned in Scripture against their own definition of holiness, love, righteousness, or some other attribute and in this way accuse God of not being truly holy, loving, or righteous. This is a classic scheme of the Devil designed to have us doubt the perfection of God through verbal or emotional manipulation. Holiness is one of God's moral attributes as well as righteousness/justice, goodness, truth, and sovereignty which we will cover in the next several chapters.

What do we mean when we say that God is holy?

To be *holy* means to cut, to separate, or to set apart. There are two senses that God is separate or set apart. Scripture presents both of these meanings of holiness: one being a broad, overall meaning and the other a specific or narrower meaning. Both are applied to God within the Scriptures. When Scripture says that God is *holy* in the broad sense, it is saying that He is *transcendent*. This is one of the most complex and incredible things about God that can be said. God's *transcendence* could and should be included in His non-moral attributes because we do not share anything in common with this attribute. When

Scripture refers to God in the narrower sense, it means that He is set apart from sin, (i.e., He is pure). It is this narrower meaning that causes this attribute to be included in the list of moral attributes which we will cover below.

What is the broad sense of God's holiness?

In the broad sense, holiness (his *transcendence*) means that God is absolutely separate from and exalted above every aspect of and part of His creation from angels, mankind, bugs, trees, atoms, space, time, natural laws, etc. He *transcends* everything, including space and time. God is above and beyond us and almost totally foreign to us. He is different than we are. We actually share very little with Him in regards to the totality of His being. Even the angels scream that He is beyond and above them.

Most often when God is called the "HOLY GOD" in Scripture, it is referring to this quality of *transcendence*. When Isaiah sees the angels proclaiming "HOLY, HOLY, HOLY!" (Isaiah 6:1-6), it is the fact that He is above all creatures and totally different from and separate from everything in power, love, mercy, or whatever else. He, in the totality of His being, cannot be compared to anything in our universe. Nothing. He is *Other*.

When God is called the "HOLY GOD" in Exodus, it is this *transcendence* being emphasized. In a sense, every attribute of God displays His holiness in that He is beyond, above, and separate from us in each area that we examine about Him.

For example, His knowledge is like ours but it is beyond ours; it is above ours and is separate from ours. It is not dependent upon ours, nor is it like ours in its scope, source, or depth. It is *holy (transcendent)* knowledge. God's holy knowledge is to our knowledge as a seven-course dinner is to dog food. It is like it, but it really isn't like it. He has knowledge to design the emotional and personality makeup of individuals in the womb (Psalm 139:13-15). Our knowledge has limits.

God even declares in Isaiah 40:18 that you can't liken God to anything: "To whom then will you liken God? Or what likeness will you compare with Him?" God's *holy* love is like our love in that it meets basic needs, but it is infinitely far beyond ours in how far it will go to meet those needs. It knows our needs at a level we can never know. His love clearly knows the difference between our needs and desires. His love is deeper, wider, higher, and longer than ours. It does not hesitate for any prejudicial reason. It is like ours, but it is really so amazing that it is not like ours at all.

God's power is like our power in that it accomplishes things and changes the course of events and people. But God's power can move a single electron or create whole worlds. He can cage the raging of the most wild beast or cunning man. He can clearly do for us what is impossible. He has power to call universes into being. He has power to adjust one sperm to go faster and create a different type of person (Psalm 139:13-15)!

In this sense, to say that God is *holy* is to say that *He is God*. It is a synonym for *deity*. It is this *otherness* of God that causes us to tremble. We are scared of ghosts and spirits because they are significantly different from us. We don't know how to predict what they will do or what rules they play by. Angels regularly appear in Scripture saying, *"Do not be afraid."* Demons seem to play on this fear and use it to try and control people. It is interesting that God does not use His transcendence to frighten people into submission. He is seeking a relational connection and worship, not terror. Bears, lions, and wild beasts frighten us because they are different. One single blow and they could kill us. God rightly accuses Job of being afraid of dinosaurs because of their size and strength and yet not being afraid of Him (Job 40:15-42:8).

We act differently around famous or powerful people because they are different from us. The trappings of majesty or importance pronounce this difference. When this difference is also magnified by an actual difference in being (as in bugs, spirits, and God), we begin to comprehend the fear of God in a new way.

Every person who has come into the presence of God has been struck down and humbled by the otherness of God. This has happened to Abraham, Moses, Isaiah, Peter, and John. There is a deep impression that there is more to God than we will ever know or understand. Some have suggested that we may be able to comprehend less than one percent of who God really is.

The Proverbs declare that the *fear of the Lord* is the beginning of wisdom. This fear is not terror but reverence tinged with a level of respect for the complete *otherness* of the being of God. We demonstrate a comprehension of God's holiness when we refuse to play around with God and the things of God.

Look up the verses that proclaim God's holiness:

Exodus 19:9-10, 16-20
Exodus 33:17-23; 34:6-8
Joshua 6:13
Isaiah 6:1-5
Ezekiel 1:4-28
Daniel 7:9-10
Matthew 17:1-6
Revelation 1:10-18
James 4:7-10

How do I take delight in God's transcendent holiness?

1. I can take delight in the holiness of God through my open submission to God and His will as the only logical choice. Many times we find ourselves angry because our plans didn't work out, never thinking that God might be changing our schedule to meet His plans. A *man plans his* *way but the Lord directs his steps* (Proverbs 16:9). We must take a real look at the talents, gifts, and opportunities that God has given us and submit to His plan for our lives. At times this must be done on a moment-by-moment basis. We believe that the best way to live our lives is by having a particular job, relationship, or large amount of money; but God clearly sends us down a different path. Can you delight in what He is asking you to do because you know that He is *holy*? His holiness has been completely factored in to who you are and His ultimate plans for your life, including how your life turns in unexpected ways to grow in holiness. Learn to submit to God openly and take delight in the way the path will turn.

2. Take delight in God's holiness by dialing back your ego and living in humility before our Transcendent God. It is foolish to project an ego field around yourself as though you were important when God is so much more than we can contemplate. Deflate the self-focus. Turn off the ego field. Humble yourself before the Holy God, and He will exalt you at the proper time. We cannot maintain arrogance or a feeling of influence if we are to really understand God. Only when you get a real glimpse of God will you be able to rise to the height of your powers with complete humility. You will constantly be aware of how much more God is than you are. Delight in the transcendence of God rather than your supposed importance.

3. Take delight in God by exploring the positive meaning of "fearing the Lord." Fearing the Lord means a reverence for God which explores incredibly deep emotions. We will one day stand on a plane of existence where we will sense the direct presence of the Almighty Transcendent God. We will be scared, loved, afraid, guilty, forgiven, unworthy, dysfunctional, and so on. Think about that time when you will be face to face with God (1 John 3:1). We can sometimes push away at the reality of eternity and our eventual presence before Him. Let your mind take you there as it says in Colossians 3:1-12 - set your mind on the things above. Take the information of the Scriptures and embrace the reality of being alive in heaven (Revelations 21,22). The Proverbs constantly talk about the fact that you will never understand life until you have a real appreciation for the awesome otherness of God. *The fear of the Lord is the beginning of wisdom* (Proverbs 9:10).

4. Take delight in the limitations that God puts on you. When the Apostle Peter says that "we are to be holy, because He is holy," he is saying that we must be willing to be set apart so that God can use us for the unique purpose He has for us. Every relationship has three elements: its benefits, its responsibilities, and its limitations. For instance, there are things I must limit in my life if I am going to have a great relationship with my wife. The same is true for God. He will ask you and me to not do some things in order to be set apart for our relationships and our specific purpose. Let me just give you a few examples. When I was seventeen years of age, I sensed that God asked me not to listen to secular music but to sing Scripture. I have embraced that limitation and God has deepened our relationship because of it. It is not for everyone, but it is for me in my relationship with God. Another example would be that I am an extremely competitive person and I find when I am playing almost any game, I want to win too badly. I have worked and worked on this and am significantly better, but eventually God has asked me to give up most competitive game situations so that I do not move over into hyper mode. This has significantly helped my testimony and my devotional relationship with God. Again, this is not a limitation that God puts on everyone; it is a personal part of my holiness. Learn to take delight in the unique limitations that your relationship with God brings to your life. Don't fight against these but instead embrace them and the depth of love that they can bring. Be careful that you do not invent holiness issues or let others put upon you their limitations. I must also add that the Devil would also like to manipulate the freedom you have in Christ with lots of religious limitations that are not really from God. The rule of thumb for each of us is to move away from sin and limit something so we can spend more time or energy pursuing God. If the limitation becomes oppressive and condemning, then it may be from the enemy and not God (Romans 8:1; Colossians 2:16-23).

What is the narrow sense of God's holiness?

In a more restricted sense, we refer to God's holiness as his complete separation from sin and moral corruption. It is in this restricted sense that God's holiness is most often associated with "sinlessness." Holiness, as separation from sin, can be thought of as the entire and complete agreement of all God's actions, thoughts, and words with His perfect will and righteousness. He never deviates in any way from what He knows is the right and just course of action. In this He is totally separate from sin. Even when He interacts with sinful beings and their sin, He deals with it in accordance with the directions of all His perfect attributes in combination.

God is totally separated from sin and impurity. He cannot be tempted by evil, nor does he tempt anyone (James 1:12-18). In virtue of God's holiness in this area, God cannot have communion with sin (Job 34:10, Habakkuk 1:13; James 1:12-16). Consistently the reaction of men to God's holiness is to notice their own impurity – like a clean sock held next to a bleached sock. The clean sock looks clean until it is compared with the pure white one (Isaiah 6:5).

It may be helpful to think of God's holiness as His absolute lack of deviation in any way from the perfect righteous standard that His wisdom and knowledge demand. He always meets the standard of doing what is right, moral, and good (taking all factors into account). The nature of good, or what is right, is what God does. If what we consider "good" is something outside of God that He must adhere to, then maybe what is good, right, and moral may change over time. But it doesn't because God doesn't change, and it is who He is that defines what is moral, good, and right.

Theoretically, we must say that God's perfection can establish the righteous standard and that God does not have to meet it. It is, however, His holiness that conforms the whole of His being and actions to the righteous and perfect standard every time. Therefore, His holiness is to be marveled at among His creatures because for us the good that we want to do, we do not do, and the evil that we seek to avoid, we do (Romans 7:19).

What has God said about Himself in regard to holiness?

Exodus 15:11; Leviticus 11:44, 19:2; Isaiah 6:1-3; 1 Peter 1:14-16

How has God manifested His holiness?

He has manifested it through statements about Himself through the Old Testament Law in all its parts and ceremonies; through critical Old and New Testament stories; through the tabernacle and the temple; through the life of the Lord Jesus; and through the church, the body of Christ.

How has God manifested His holiness in the Old Testament Law?

In order to comprehend the Old Testament, it is critical to see it in the light of God's holiness. The whole thrust of God's commands to the Jews was to be a holy nation, a nation set apart (Leviticus 19). The Jews were to be the zenith of perfection in every area of life. They were to be totally separated from any mixture.

God's commands to the Jews have been divided into three separate categories: the moral law, the ceremonial, and the civil law. These divisions do not appear in Scripture but are a helpful way of understanding the laws God gave. The moral law is what we call the Ten Commandments. These commands form the basis of what God expects from us as the basic requirements for separation from sin. The Ten Commandments are given largely in the negative to stress what to stay away from. The most important moral directive is that we are to love. They put a boundary around the definition of love - *You shall love the Lord your God with all your heart, soul, mind, and strength, and your neighbor as yourself.* The Ten Commandments tell us definitively what is not love. You cannot call it love when you have a wife and an adulteress relationship with another woman. You can't call it love when you steal someone else's goods. You can't call it love when you dishonor those in authority over you. The positive aspects of the ideas were stated in the Old Testament, but they waited for Christ to give them full exploration and manifestation.

The civil law is God's application of the Ten Commandments to everyday life. You had to put a guardrail on your roof so that you did not accidentally break the commandment not to kill. You were to notify your neighbor within a certain number of days if one of their animals wandered into your area lest you violate the commandment not to steal. All these applications are God-given illustrations on how to apply the Ten Commandments to a civil society. We have these kinds of laws now – we call them ordinances, codes, rules, or laws. They apply very specifically the truths of the Ten Commandments to situations in our lives.

The ceremonial laws were the purification laws regarding disease, menstruation, ejaculation, washing the dead and other items, food, and clothing. These ceremonial laws were designed by God to teach the absolute separation of the holy with the profane. Certain types of animals were not eaten because they were not perfect representatives of their grouping. The dead were not to be touched because this was not a normal or perfect condition. Those infected with disease were different and needed to be excluded from the commonwealth of Israel. We do not follow these laws today because Christ has come; we do not need to teach in shadowy pictures when the reality is present. We are a holy nation in the real sense. God declared all foods clean and the time of using the food laws, the clothing laws, and the other symbol-laden laws is over because Jesus Christ, the Light of the World, is here.

The ceremonial laws also include the sin offerings, burnt offerings, thank offerings, and the whole process of being forgiven for sins committed. Christ has completely forgiven our sins by His death on the cross; therefore, we do not need to deal with illustrations any more (Hebrews 8:1-13). Christ fulfilled the Law and became the sacrifice for our sins; He is our whole burnt offering and our thank offering. Every part of the old sacrificial system is fulfilled in Christ Jesus' life, death, and resurrection.

What critical stories teach us about God's holiness?

There are many biblical stories that tell of God's holiness and the seriousness to which it is to be taken. In the story of Nadab and Abihu in Leviticus 10:1-7, the sons of Aaron offered a different type of incense to the Lord than He had prescribed. They were slain on the spot for not treating God as holy.

In the story of Phineas and the intermarried couple (Numbers 26:1-13), God's anger had broken out among the people of Israel because of their intermarriages with pagans which led to idolatry and immoral practices. A plague was sweeping through the population. God ordered that the judges of Israel kill those polluting the nation. Moses commanded the leaders to act. Phineas saw an Israeli leader bring a Midianite woman into the camp. He thrust them through with a spear in the midst of relations and received God's commendation.

The story of Uzzah and the tipping of the ark in 2 Samuel 6:1-11 tells of how David sought to move the Ark of the Covenant to the new capital city, Jerusalem. They put the Ark on an oxcart against God's written instruction. When it threatened to fall off, Uzzah reached out to steady it and God slayed him almost instantly. It made everyone afraid of God and stopped the procession.

In the story of Ananias and Sapphira and the offering plate told in Acts 5:1-13 and 8:1-13, the lesson is that God is not to be treated with a lack of respect. He is very exact and demands our obedience. He teaches that He is holy. Each of these stories is designed to teach that God is not like us. He does not just overlook a small mistake or a good try.

How has the Lord demonstrated His holiness in the tabernacle and the temple?

Another demonstration of God's holiness is the specific details in the way He was to be worshipped in the tabernacle and the temple. He made these areas completely separate from the people. He put high walls and rooms within rooms to protect the people from His presence. He made a progression of washing and purification as one would get closer to God. All of the pieces and articles of the tabernacle and temple were of non-ordinary or special material. The whole of the building was different and set apart from the average because it housed the completely set-apart (holy) One.

How does the life of the Lord Jesus manifest God's holiness?

From His birth to His death, Jesus was different. He was born of a virgin. He lived a sinless life. He went in among the sinners and the diseased and infected them instead of the other way around. He changed the world through twelve average men and a handful of women. He willingly gave up His life for those who were not worthy of His support. He rose from the dead to prove that what He said was true. Jesus was in every way different and set apart as the unique man. He is holy in every sense of the word.

How does the church display the holiness of God?

The church is the unique and special creation of God, which is totally different from any other organization in this world. The church is the collection of those who have willingly become slaves to the Lord Jesus. Each individual in the true church went through a rebirth experience to initiate them into this group. The church is the collection of those who know that they are sinners and undeserving of His love. The church crosses every prejudicial barrier ever erected and causes mankind to truly love each other.

How does God's ethical, set-apart holiness affect my life? How can I delight in this sense of God's holiness?

1. I can take delight in God's holiness by getting ready for worship, by confessing my sin, and becoming separate from my selfishness (Psalm 29:2; Psalm 96:9; Joshua 24:19). We must be attired in holiness (separated from sin) if our worship is to be effective and honoring. We cannot expect God to be pleased with our gifts of praise and offerings if we are not willing to cleanse the sinfulness from our minds, actions, and hearts. We must not degrade God with our ascriptions to Him or our assumptions about Him. We cannot begin to think that God is just like us because He is not. He does not wink or ignore sin. The Devil wants us to be too afraid of God to approach Him or to be so shamed by our sin that we do not accept His forgiveness. Remember that God wants us to be holy, but God is who cleanses us from our lack of holiness. So come to God and admit you are not holy so that you can be cleansed through forgiveness and become more set apart to Him. I must regularly examine my life to see what sins I have committed. The Holy God will not dwell long with the unholy. I must be willing to move away from that which God declares to be wrong, immoral, or unfit. It does not matter whether it is popular in my culture. Understand that regular repentance is a part of the normal Christian life.

2. I can take delight in the holiness of God by realizing that God has a path laid out for me that is full of "God works" (Ephesians 1:4; 2:10). God has a path laid out for me, and it doesn't matter how far from the path I have wandered. He has issued forward a path that I am to follow. It is that path that will result in my being pleasing to Him. It is that path that will result in the greatest joy without sorrow in the present and in the future. We can often see clearly where the selfish paths lead and where God's path leads. Take delight in God's path by getting on it and refusing to get off of it. I am to be separate from all the selfish desires that regularly suggest themselves to me. Recognize the difference between the selfishness that lives within you and the part of you that wants to follow God. Let the God-follower part of you win.

3. I can take delight in God by changing from what my old desires wanted to do into a replica of God, the Holy One (1 Peter 1:14-16; 2 Corinthians 3:17,18). There is a supernatural process at work in those who are Christians. It transforms them to be more holy as they pursue and gaze at Christ. They become like the One they are pursuing. God wants us to allow this transformation process to take place. At first it seems weird or strange to no longer enjoy or want some of the things that occupied our lives. We become willing to change our dress, our hair, our speech, and our behavior in order to be more like what is happening on the inside.

4. I can take delight that God will take whatever means He deems necessary to get us to stop living out our old life (2 Corinthians 4:7-11; Romans 8:28,29). God is not as concerned about whether we are outwardly prosperous or outwardly "happy." He is far more concerned about whether we are making spiritual progress and are blessed. It is the blessing of God that allows us to enjoy the outward prosperity and happiness. What God puts us through or allows us to go through is like a school that is designed to teach us to handle things from a spiritual point of view. We are to become more able to handle the obstacles, problems, and difficulties of life by living in a deeper spiritual perspective. When God points out something that is wrong in our lives, we must be willing to get rid of it. When the Holy Spirit convicts us that an activity – while not wrong – takes our time and energy away from more vital interests, we must be willing to prune the suckers from the trunk. It is true that often God Himself prunes activities or useless pursuits through lack of funds, disasters, health concerns, and the like; but it seems that God only does this when we are not sensitive to His still small voice saying that we should re-examine our involvement. (1 Corinthians 11:31 says that if we judged ourselves rightly, we should not be judged; 1 Peter 3:14; 1 John 3:2-3).

5. I can take delight that I stand out to former friends and acquaintances as I pursue God's will primarily (1 Peter 4:1-4). When Christians get serious about following God, they begin to look and act different from their friends. This process can cause some to back away from the changes that God is seeking to make. It is essential, however, that God be allowed to separate us from those who are not really pursuing God. Often those who are only lukewarm in their faith are the greatest impediment to our growing faith. It is better to be a zealous Christian than to just waste away in ambivalent mediocrity.

Chapter 11
His Attributes:
He is Righteous and Just

What do we mean by the righteousness of God?

By righteousness we mean the divine standard which comes from God as to what is good, acceptable, and perfect (Romans 12:2). God is the very definition of what is right. To say that God conforms His actions and character to that standard is to say that He is righteous.

Where does this standard come from to which God must adhere?

Let's spend just a few moments thinking about where our standard of right and wrong comes from. This discussion can sound like philosophy, but it is really crucial in our delighting in God. This discussion has been the source of serious errors in theology and societal problems. If we do not know where our standard of morality comes from, then it can lead to the destruction of communities and even nations. (It already has!) Does it come from the will of God? In other words, does God arbitrarily say what is right and what is wrong even though He himself may not always do it? Is what God declares "right" simply an arbitrary standard that may change if God wants it to change?

Another option for where the standard of righteousness comes from in our universe is that it comes from something behind God or a standard to which God himself must adhere. If this were the case, then there is a God behind God or something that is more powerful than God. The Scriptures clearly state that this is not the case, so the standard of righteousness that is evidenced by God's actions and judgments come from the perfections of His being (Isaiah 43:10-11). God being Himself is the living embodiment of the righteousness that He asks of us.

When we say that the standard of right and wrong come from the perfections of God, we mean that all the attributes of God combine to establish that which is the proper response in any given situation. His wisdom, knowledge, power, presence, grace, mercy, goodness, holiness, and sovereignty combine to define righteousness in any given situation (Exodus 34:6,7).

This suggests that the standard to which God's righteousness always adheres is limited by the compilation of the perfections of His nature. Any overemphasis of a particular attribute of God can make God look like a monster, a weakling, non-existent, and/or can result in our believing that we are gods ourselves. If we are to understand God in righteous delight, we will understand God as a whole, not in fragmented parts. This understanding answers those difficult questions like, "If God were a loving God, how could He let all these innocent people suffer?"

Does God have a standard for each of His creatures including Himself?

Yes. From the lowest plants to mammals – including man and angels – each one of the standards is slightly different (Genesis 1:1-31). Only mankind and angels have the opportunity to personally opt out of meeting the standard of God for their kind. These standards are the basis of what that kind is to do to glorify God and fulfill its purpose in life. Fish are to swim. Birds are to fly. Insects are to devour the refuse. Each kind is to reproduce after its kind. Mankind is to glorify God through their talents and enjoy God forever.

What is God's standard for mankind?

God has given one standard of righteousness, but it can be divided into two general categories. These standards of righteousness are what He expects from humans. These also form a blueprint on how to live and set up a civilization.

1. What He expects of us in relation to Himself.

2. What He expects of us in relation to others.

Both of these two lists of expectations are contained in a negative way in the Ten Commandments. They are declared positively in the two Great Commandments. It is unfortunate that the Ten Commandments have fallen out of favor in America for they formed the basis of the legal system and were the foundation of a society that championed new incredible freedoms. Those freedoms will not be able to be maintained without a common submission to the Ten Commandments of God.

God's Commandments in relation to Himself:

You shall have no other God's before Me." (Exodus 20:3)

You shall make no idols...neither to worship them, nor to serve them. (Exodus 20:4-6)

You shall not take the name of the Lord thy God in vain. (Exodus 20:7)

Remember the Sabbath day to keep it holy. (Exodus 20:8)

God's Commandments in relation to others:

Honor thy Father and thy Mother... (Exodus 20:12)

You shall not murder. (Exodus 20:13)

You shall not commit adultery. (Exodus 20:14)

You shall not steal. (Exodus 20:16)

You shall not bear false witness against thy neighbor. (Exodus 20:16)

You shall not covet. (Exodus 20:17)

These ten dimensions of the standard that God has given to mankind are detailed in the negative to suggest the minimum that God will accept as righteous. While these standards are not specific enough to derive detailed law codes, these are to form the basis on which the legal codes of a society are built. It is when we find a civilization passing laws that do the opposite of these standards that the walls of the society begin to crumble. When a culture begins to ignore God's standard and adopt their own, the culture begins the downward spiral into the slavery of sin and destruction.

What does the righteousness of God mean to me? How can I take delight in God's righteous standards?

1. I can take delight in God's righteousness when I remember that God will always think certain things are wrong and certain things are right (Hebrews 13:8). God does not change His standards. We can be sure that the things God delights in today are what He took delight in during Abraham's day or Elijah's day. What God found wrong and abhorrent in biblical times, He still finds revolting today. It is a shame that people want to suggest that the standards of the Bible do not apply because this is a modern time. God has not changed and people have basically not changed. The only thing that has changed is the technology, which puts greater strains upon our relationships. We need God's lines and standards today more than ever.

2. I can take delight in God's righteousness when I remember that God will never be arbitrary about any of His actions or decisions. When He acts or fails to act, I can seek God's face as to what to do in any situation. I can realize He is allowing me to face this for a reason, and He has a right way to handle this particular problem. Also, some situations require prayer, choices, and other actions in order to achieve a righteous solution. It is never that God was backed into a corner or just because He wanted to do it that way. I can be confident that God has

He is Righteous and Just

considered the possibilities that I am facing. He allowed me to confront my particular problem because the perfections of His being dictated that it was best for me to face this problem. I realize that many times I put myself in a difficult situation because of my foolish choices or that others I am around make unwise or immoral choices.

3. I can take delight in God's righteousness when I remember that I have a minimum standard to measure myself against: the Ten Commandments. If our world is going to begin to become the better place that all people hope it will be, then it must be willing to set up a minimum standard. Right now there are technologies that are beginning to set up minimum standards for sharing data and working together. As people, we need to come to terms with minimum standards of conduct. Only in that way will we be able interact without the petty jealousy and factionalism that we are now seeing.

4. I can take delight in God's righteousness when I remember that there are absolutes. Given the same set of circumstances, the right response will always be the same. It is important to say in an intelligent discussion of absolutes that the Ten Commandments are absolutes in the same circumstances and situations. At times, in the past, it has been maintained that the Ten Commandments are absolute in every situation and in every case. It is this thinking that suggests that the Sixth Commandment outlaws capital punishment. The Sixth Commandment clearly outlaws murder and its preliminaries of violence, physical harm, etc. It cannot, however, be applied to every act of physical harm or death; or it makes God at war with his own standard for demanding the death of certain individuals.

The same can be said about the Ninth Commandment. This has been suggested as an absolute and it is. But there are three ways of moving close to a violation of "You shall not bear false witness against your neighbor" and yet not violating it. It is possible to bear false witness neither against, nor for, your neighbor as in the case of a drama or play or film. The events in a fictionalized play are clearly false but do not violate this command. Second, it is possible to bear false witness for your neighbor as in the situation of Nathan trying to get David to realize he had sinned against God by telling him a story. Third, it is possible to bear false witness against an enemy as in the case of Rahab telling the enemies of God that the spies had already gone out of the city. It is sufficient to delight in the absolutes of God, realizing that it is important to think hard and clearly about when and where and how those absolutes apply. God has not left us in the dark. He has given us the Scriptures to guide us and show us how He wants them applied. It is unfortunate that a simplistic application of the commandments in the past has caused them to be discarded in the present. The result is that our society is floundering, trying to find its moorings. We must return again to God's righteous standards for conduct.

He is Righteous and Just

5. I can take delight in God's righteousness when I remember that God could not just pardon sinners because He wanted to. He has to satisfy the demands of righteousness. Many believe that God is in the forgiveness business. "Oh, God will forgive; it's his job!" God is righteous and must punish sin (Ezekiel 18:4). The soul that sins will die. There is a truth built into the warp and woof of the universe— that which violates the laws God has set up will run down, decay, and will eventually need to be destroyed. God's forgiveness of our violations of His laws comes only because God in His infinite wisdom identified a way to meet the demands of justice, while at the same time preserving those who embrace His way. The demands of justice that emanate from God were not and cannot be discarded but were explored and sacrificially met. The requirements of the laws of God were met in the sacrifice of Jesus Christ on the Cross and are applied through our belief of Him.

6. I can take delight in God's righteousness when I remember that God has been compassionate to tell us the standard and not to make us guess about the standard. God has clearly declared the standard that He measures humanity against. It is that standard that clearly helps us see our need for a Savior. Any person who takes a serious look at the demands of the Ten Commandments sees that they need a Savior for they fall short of them. The standard drives us to the Savior (Galatians 3:24).

7. I can take delight in God's righteousness when I remember that we have a blueprint on how to make society work. God invented the whole of creation so He knows how it should run. The creation runs on the laws of physics and biology. These laws are only just now being remotely understood. However, the crown of God's creation was given the opportunity to stay within the lines of God's moral law. We have, in every case, colored outside of the lines. We have gone beyond the boundaries that God has set for us. It is significant that God has not left us without a plan on how to operate our society in the best possible way in light of the sinful nature of man. It has often been said that God's laws are much more restrictive than we might make on our own or that they are more restrictive than they need to be. What becomes plainly obvious to anyone who looks at the historical evidence – as well as the medical, psychological, social, emotional, and relational evidence of the present – is that putting the restrictions in any other place destroys someone or something. For example, to suggest that sexuality ought to be confined to a committed relationship solely seems restrictive and dull. But now it is seen that to open up one's relationships to free love destroys not only real love but also the children of those who are experimenting.

THE JUSTICE OF GOD

Having gone over that God has a standard of conduct that defines right and wrong, one can now properly talk about the justice of God. The justice of God is how God behaves towards His creatures as they relate to His standard.

There are two types of justice:

1. **Positive justice: rewards and blessing**

2. **Negative justice: punishment or retribution**

God exhibits both kinds of justice – positive and negative.

Positive Justice

God rewards the smallest righteous or obedient action with blessings above the return on the action. This includes an immediate reward or blessing as well as an ultimate reward or blessing.

Immediate: Deuteronomy 7:9,12,13; Psalm 68:11; Micah 7:20; Matthew 8:3-12; Hebrews 11:24-27

God has promised to reward and bless our obedience to His laws and principles. If He did not, He would not be just.

Some have mistakenly suggested that this blessing from righteous actions includes salvation from sins. No, being saved is a gift of His grace, and it is not earned or deserved. It is a gift. You can't pay for a gift.

This has also mistakenly led to the idea that one righteous action cancels out one unrighteous action. It is the idea that there is a cosmic scale somewhere with good on one side and bad on the other. Taking the trash out does not affect that I threw a rock through the neighbor's window.

Another mistaken idea is that God's blessing for righteous actions is material or monetary. Nowhere in Scripture does God promise that material or monetary blessings have to follow from righteousness (except in regard to Israel keeping the whole law). That righteous actions often are followed by material and monetary rewards is God's willingness to work with our stupidity and weakness (spiritual blessings are more desirable – see Ephesians 1).

Ultimate: Matthew 25:21; Romans 2:7

There is a sense in which our entrance into heaven will be a demonstration of the outworking of our belief. James says that faith alone without works is dead. The passage in Romans suggests that God will say, "Great, you say you believe in Jesus! What do you present as evidence that your belief is real?" Another way of saying this: God will say, "Talk is cheap! I want to look at your life and see if the Fruit of the Spirit was produced."

He is Righteous and Just

The person who is thinking clearly knows that God's blessings and grace for doing what we are told is completely unmerited.

Negative Justice

God brings a punishment upon every act of wickedness or disobedience. This includes an immediate consequence or punishment as well as an ultimate consequence or punishment.

Immediate: Proverbs 1:23; Romans 1:18; Romans 2:5,6; Romans 12:17-19

This is true in spite of the fact that many people look as though they are getting away with sin and wickedness. Many have just accepted God's reproofs as the normal expected results of living. We have abandoned a belief in a cause-and-effect universe for one that is random and absurd. One cannot live like that, so we selectively attach justice to individual parts of the universe. It would be better to go back and begin to believe in the universe that God made – one where every effect has a cause. Righteousness begets righteousness and wickedness begets wickedness (Psalm 37:3-7).

Ultimate: 2 Thessalonians 1:6-8; Romans 2:6,7

There is a sense in which God will judge not only each individual act we commit but the whole of our lives and the direction it is headed. Not only will justice only be served as each action is evaluated but also in what could have been done with the time and the confirmed direction of the heart. God is able to extrapolate out based upon the tiny fraction of actions your life constitutes.

How can I delight in God's righteousness and justice?

1. I can take delight that my righteous choices receive God's blessing beyond their merit. God not only gives me temporal credit for my right choices (He allows me to enjoy the good consequences of my right choices). He also seems to be especially pleased (giving some form of spiritual rewards or credit) for doing what I should have done (1 Thessalonians 4:1-3; 2 Timothy 4:7,8; 1 Corinthians 3:12-14).

2. I can take delight in God's righteousness in that my righteous choices lead to more righteous choices which were not available before I made the first one. This is one of the blessings of righteousness. Every right choice leads to more right choices. It is one of the blessings of righteousness and the curses of wickedness. Each time I make a wrong choice, I not only suffer the consequences of that bad choice; but I also miss out on the blessings from the righteous choice. On the other side, the opposite is also true. If I make the righteous choice, then I not only enjoy the benefit of the righteous choice; but I also avoid the reproof of the wrong choice. In effect, every choice I make has a double blessing or penalty attached to it.

The other aspect of righteous choices and wicked choices is that all the positive rewards of wickedness are front-loaded. One receives all the benefits of a wicked choice right away (that is why they are enticing) while righteous choices are like investing in a bank the benefits come after time. Living a life of righteousness grows in its rewards over time (Psalm 37:3-11). God is blessing us for each righteous choice and allowing us to suffer the consequences of our wicked choices.

It is important to remember that each righteous choice has a double blessing. In this way it is possible to rather quickly desire to change your life and move away from the sewer of wickedness. This is also how it is possible for a good person to move deep into wickedness quickly.

3. I can take delight in the righteousness of God in every area of life and know that in this relationship it is impossible to earn God's favor and rewards (ultimate righteousness). It is a gift and is not earned or deserved (Ephesians 2:8,9). That God is righteous, rather than arbitrary, means someone can enjoy the blessings of God in parts of their life and not be going to heaven. This is because they do not have ultimate righteousness which comes by faith alone. It is not earned or bought. There are people who have not embraced the gift of ultimate righteousness, but they have discovered God's principles in some other area of their life. God rewards righteous behavior in each area of life. Because it is impossible to earn or deserve ultimate righteousness, He gives it to us as a gift that is received through faith. There are some non-Christians who have better marriages or closer family ties than Christians. They are following God's principles even though they might not recognize them as God's principles. God has universal righteous principles in each of our relationships: God, Personal Development, Marriage, Family, Work, Church, Money, Friends, Society. It is our relationship with God that determines whether or not we are on our way to heaven. So it is possible for someone to be using God's principles in the other areas of life and have a pretty good life.

4. I can take delight in the perfect righteousness of God in that a Christian, who is bound for heaven because of their dependence on God, can still suffer reproof or consequences from God for any rebellious, ignorant, or deceived ways. We need to constantly grow so that we will be in line with God's righteousness in every relationship and suffer the reproofs of God less and less. It is important that Christians realize that they are called *disciples or learners* for a reason. Christians have committed themselves to learning God's righteous standards and living by them with all the strength that God supplies. God's consequences, justice, and wrath will move out against even those bound for heaven. Christians do not suffer His ultimate wrath, but they can still suffer consequences in this life for unrighteous behavior (Proverbs 1:20-23).

5. It means that my wrong choices expose me to the aspects of the justice of God in an immediate sense which includes the deception of Satan. Just because a person has accepted God's gift of ultimate righteousness through faith, it is possible for them to sin and suffer the consequences for that. The Apostle Paul says that one's choices may be so wrong that one can be handed over to the Devil to be taught not to blaspheme (1 Corinthians 5:5). We must not believe that just because a person is a Christian they are exempted from the consequences of wrong or the wrath of God in its immediate sense. In fact, God will be more involved in the life of those whom he loves than the non-Christian (Hebrews 12:6,10).

6. I can take delight in the righteousness of God and His love for me for His righteousness is the reason why He had to go to the trouble of incarnating the Son, letting Him suffer the ignominy of living as a man, and allowing Him to be rejected and killed. God must be just. He cannot be loving without justice being properly served. While our society has abandoned a strict sense of justice, God cannot (2 Corinthians 5:19-21). Even our society is paying a just price for its abandonment of righteousness. We can ponder other ways to build a world or a society, but the infinite God – who through the perfections of His being and after examining all the possibilities of various worlds and interactions between creatures – has instilled the present system of justice and created the world. Through that perfect system of justice, God found that only through His own Son's life and death could mankind be redeemed without destroying justice or letting every person suffer the torment of hell. Marvel in the wonder of God who would suffer so much to love and redeem you.

7. I can take delight in God's righteousness and justice in that Christ's death on the cross was the only way for man to be redeemed. Jesus pleaded with God the Father for some other way to redeem mankind: Could God please take that way? The Almighty, Omniscient, righteous God did not change his course, so this was the only way. If there were another way to achieve the salvation of mankind, God the Father would have moved heaven and earth to bring it about at the request of his Son. Since the Father allowed the Son's request to fall on "deaf ears," Christ understood that there was no other way to bring about the redemption of mankind. Jesus said in the garden, "Father, let this cup pass from me." Look deep at the incredible love and righteousness that meet in the death of Christ.

Chapter 12
His Attributes:
He is Good

What is the "Goodness of God"? What do we mean when we call God good?

There are two aspects to God's goodness. One is the overarching philosophical definition of goodness and the other is the moral or ethical aspect of goodness. The overarching philosophical definition of goodness is *that which answers to perfection or complete conformity to the ideal.*

And He said, "I Myself will make all My goodness pass before you, and will proclaim the name of the LORD before you; and I will be gracious to whom I will be gracious, and will show compassion on whom I will show compassion" (Exodus 33:19).

God is in every way good in this sense.

We have, however, rendered our discussion on this sense in regard to the holiness and righteousness of God. It is interesting that when God actually passed by Moses, it was in both senses of His goodness that He passed by. Moses became aware of the fact that God is total goodness and particular goodness for His creatures. It is that personal or particular goodness that Moses relied upon.

Then the LORD passed by in front of him and proclaimed, "The LORD, the LORD God, compassionate and gracious, slow to anger, and abounding in lovingkindness and truth" (Exodus 34:6).

What do we mean when we call God "good" in the moral or ethical sense?

It is the perfection of God's being which causes Him to...

1. ...deal bountifully with His creatures. God has bestowed upon His creatures incredible bounty. It is possible to become ungrateful surrounded by presents or gifts. Psychologists tell us that we can become used to almost anything after twenty-eight days. We begin to take for granted the things that we have been exposed to for over a month. This is why we seem to overlook that God has supplied us with a wonderful planet full of life. He has given us food, air, water, friends, parents, material possessions, etc. He has also endowed us with the abilities that allow us to get along in the world: mental faculties, physical abilities, emotional reactions, spiritual senses, specialized abilities, dreams, talents, and gifts. God has truly dealt bountifully with His creatures. It is very helpful to remember all the good things that God has given us that allow us to exist (James 1:17). We also must understand that the evil that is the destroyer of God's good gifts comes from man and his choices.

He is Good

2. ...do what is best for His creatures. God also does what is best for His creatures in that He can see both the future as well as the imaginations of our hearts. He moves to provide that which will be best in the long haul for His creatures. We are often only concerned in that which is pleasurable in the short run. God makes His will clear to those who really want to know it. God provides what will meet the needs of His creatures as well as comforts. He does not give gifts that will boomerang and destroy when they started out good. It is important that God supplies that which is best for His creatures and He withholds things and directions that would not be the best for them. Many a Christian has cursed God for not allowing them to do a particular thing that they could not see was wrong at the time. But the goodness of God does not allow Him to give a package of razor blades to His children even if they want them and are wrapped in a pretty package (Psalm 8:4-9; Matthew 7:11).

He is the source of all good.

That God is good means that He is the source of everything that is good. He defines what is good for each creature and then He supplies those things for His creatures. What God supplies is beneficial and non-destructive. Because of sin it is possible for us to find that which gives us pleasure but is not beneficial. Much sin is a twisting or perversion of something good so that a selfish pleasure can be gained. We suffer the consequences of those foolish spurts of pleasure. God is the source and definition of good. Never forget that there is nothing that is beneficial to be gained by going outside of His law and will. It may be momentarily pleasurable, but it is not good (James 1:17; Deuteronomy 30:9; Psalm 36:9).

Any discussion of good or God's goodness must stem from the idea that everything good in our lives comes from God. Every good thing we have – including life itself – is from God (James 1:17). Some see the blessings or good gifts of God as bad. This needs to be labeled as aberrant thinking. Life is a good gift, suicide is not good; marriage is a gift, adultery is not good; government is a gift, anarchy is not good. Some take for granted the multitudinous good gifts of God and keep looking for more or new gifts. Some would define goodness as pleasure, which is something that God does not do. Some would even deny that God is good if He does not meet their latest desire.

He is the highest good to which a creature can seek. (Psalm 34:8-10; 36:9; 2 Chronicles 6:13; Jeremiah 9:23; Psalm 104:21; Hosea 3:5; Mark 10:18)

Since He is the perfection of all, we find in Him every personal, emotional, and mental connection that fills us up. He is the source and when we arrive at Him, we find our rest. Is it possible to break down the blinding brilliance of God's goodness into rays of color that are easier to understand? Yes. The four aspects of God's goodness are His love, His grace, His mercy, and His longsuffering.

He is Good

1. His love is the perfection of being that meets needs, pursues, and pleases His creatures. (2 Chronicles 7:3; Psalm 25:8-11; Psalm 33:8; Psalm 86:6; John 3:16; 1 John 3:1; Luke 6:35-38) It is important to realize that God calls us to be like Him in His goodness. He wants us to benefit and care for others. His goodness is not just to flow to us; it must flow through us. This is when we are most Christ-like. Some people do not wish to be loved. God is not in the habit of forcing His love on undeserving subjects. He does meet the basic needs of His subjects so that they might be sustained long enough to desire that He love them more. We, as well as all creatures, are full of needs which we must have God meet. He is moved in the depth of His being to meet these needs. We need to remember that this aspect of His being is demonstrated in the perfect combination of all of His other attributes. We cannot isolate this attribute and demand that God must act in a certain way.

2. His grace is that perfection of His being which provides for and bestows favor, blessing, power, gifts, and love upon the undeserving. (Matthew 5:44-47; Romans 6:1-8; Ephesians 2:8-9) This involves meeting basic needs, desires, and uncontemplated blessings. We need to understand that God's grace is something we do not deserve but that we must respond to or it does us no good (Hebrews 12:18). Our response to the grace of God determines the level of blessing and favor of God in our life.

3. His mercy is that perfection of His being which provides for and bestows blessing, support, and favor upon those who are afflicted, in distress, or misery regardless of how they came to be in that state. (Exodus 20:2; Deuteronomy 7:9; Psalm 86:8; Luke 1:60) He bestows mercy on those who ask with a penitent heart. God's job is not to be merciful, but it is an attribute of His character that He is this way. It is also true that His justice demands that we be penitent to activate the ever-present mercy of God. The mercy of God will be present at judgment day (Revelation 20:11-15), but no one will sincerely take advantage of it. They will be too full of themselves. Their choice was at an earlier time (when they were alive).

4. His longsuffering is that perfection of His being which bears with the disobedience, rebellion, and evil of His creatures and gives them time to repent before the righteous judgment of God falls. (Genesis 6:3) God has a limit to His longsuffering; He will not suffer forever with fools and sinners. Prior to the flood, however, He gave ample time and means for mankind to repent. He does this today as well. Given the righteousness of God, it is amazing that He is able to hold off the judgment that is due for so long. We must understand His longsuffering in the light of His holiness and righteousness. Many people presume on the longsuffering of God as though this were His only attribute. They believe that because God has held off this long, He will always hold off (2 Peter 3:3-9). Some mistakenly believe God does not really care about sin and foolishness. Nothing could be further from the truth. There is a need to quake with fear before the Almighty who has stored up His wrath and judgment this long. It is, in fact, the heart's cry of the righteous that God would come to the end of His longsuffering and rise up as judge of the whole earth and dispense with the wicked (Psalm 94:1-8).

Now lest we become enamored with the opposite of God's longsuffering, we need to spend time exploring and examining the wonder of God's patience with fools and sinners (Exodus 34:6; Psalm 86:15; Psalm 68:19; Romans 2:4; 9:22; 1 Peter 3:20; 2 Peter 3:15). The wrath of God is coming and will fall when the limits of God's patience have been reached. This means that when God's righteousness and holiness can no longer justify the putting off of the full consequences of sin, His wrath will fall. The truly remarkable thing is that God is so longsuffering given His absolute holiness. It suggests that we must be more patient with the ignorance and shortcomings of our fellow Christians.

How can I take delight in God's goodness?

1. I can take delight in God's goodness by acknowledging, reciting, and enjoying the ways that God is being good right now. He is being good, but we are often willfully ignorant because we are singularly focused on some pleasure or desire. Step back and see the bigger picture. How is God being good to you right now? Figure it out!

2. I can take delight that God is loving me right now. God is seeking to meet my needs and pursue me as a person, not just as a creature. He is also seeking to please me with special little blessings that are meaningful to me. My ability to enjoy and experience the wonder of God's love seems to be my willingness to let Him love me. Many times I turn away from His love because it does not seem like love, or because I am more interested in pursuing what I think is a need than what God wants me to do.

3. I can take delight in God's goodness in that I know that God is right now being merciful to me. Each and every day God could in a completely just way eliminate me from my present existence for my sins of omission and commission. It is God's mercy that sustains me. At times it is helpful to catch a glimpse of the sinful wickedness that lives within even the most pure person. It is God's mercy that allows me to live, move, and exist.

4. I can take great delight in the goodness of God that He is right now waiting with longsuffering and patience not only for me but also for the whole world. There will come a time when the waiting will be over and He will reach back into the universe that He created in a way that will demonstrate His control over it. He will say, "Enough of this sin and depravity! It is time to make things right again."

5. **I can delight in God's grace which allows me to overlook the hurts, wounds, and obstacles that others put in my path.** God grants His grace to me constantly (His power and desire) in order to not throw a tantrum over what happens to me. I need to respond to the grace of God or a root of bitterness will spring up and defile many (Hebrews 12:16).

6. **God is benefiting my community, my country, my family, my church, and me. It would be foolish to turn away from His benevolence and try to live on my own.** Delight in the wonder of all of these benefits. See them, count them, enjoy them. I need to acknowledge the consistent goodness of God coming in my direction and seek to move in accordance with it rather than my own feelings or sinful desires.

7. **I can count on – and even call out – the goodness of God in the midst of my trials and in this way delight in God even when in pain.** He is patient with me and is ready to forgive my sinfulness. I am able to embrace the lovingkindness and benefits of God even before I have them. I can claim them. I know that God is waiting and wanting to be good to me. I know that He is at present being good to me.

8. **I realize that if God continually blocks something that I want to do, then He is trying to benefit me.** I may not completely understand or cooperate with His plan, but

I will learn to delight in this blocked "blessing." I must make sure that I pray, work, and walk in the "now" of what God is doing in my life. I can choose a future in my mind that would not really be good for me. If I walk in the light with Christ, then I can be confident that God will block my advancement down a detrimental path even though I think it is necessary and important.

Chapter 13
His Attributes: He is Sovereign

We have come to the last of the attributes of God – His sovereignty. We have examined His Omniscience, Omnipotence, Omnipresence, Immutability, Holiness, Righteousness/Justice, and Goodness. There are many more attributes, aspects, and depths to God that have not and cannot be explored in this volume. The wonder of God is inexhaustible. But now let us launch into His sovereignty. This attribute needs special focus because of its critical function within the Godhead. It also needs special focus because of a lack of understanding in our day and age as well as the extreme views of the past. If our discussion of God's sovereignty is not thoroughly biblical, then heresy and significant error always result. In fact, an inaccurate discussion of God's sovereignty can actually push people away from the beauty, wonder, and majesty of God.

What do we mean when we describe God as sovereign?

We mean that God is King over the whole universe. God is sovereign. He is the owner of all things. He has the absolute right to rule His creation, and He does exercise authority over His creation. He has not started the creation and then let it run itself. He is actively involved in the preservation and direction of the universe and history.

The truth that God is sovereign is one of the most precious doctrines of the Christian faith. It can provide tremendous comfort and peace. A great theologian of the past remarked, "They rejoice that the Lord God omnipotent reignth; that neither necessity, not chance, not folly of man, nor the malice of Satan controls the sequence of events and all their issues." (Charles Hodge, *Systematic Theology*, "Sovereignty")

To realize that God is sovereign means that we do not have to try and play God. Those things that are not in our control are in the hands of a loving God. It means that worry can be abandoned and replaced by analysis and peace.

Why do we say that God is Sovereign?

Because His love, grace, goodness, power, wisdom, knowledge, presence, holiness, and all the aspects of His being combine to place Him as sovereign and direct His every action and decision as sovereign. In other words, He does not make some decisions that are unloving or some decisions that are unwise or unrighteous. All of His decisions grow out of the totality of who He is (Ephesians 1:11). Yes, there are decisions that He has clearly made where we would wonder why He has not leaned into His love or mercy more, but some aspect of His being is informing His love that it is not wise to do that. Some wonder why God has not brought condemnation or justice to the wicked sooner; and yet God's love, holiness, and longsuffering inform His righteous justice that it is not yet time. It is because of all that He is that He is sovereign. Any other being trying to be God of the universe would be a monster – as evidenced by the Devil's destructive rebellion. If His sovereignty were based upon His will alone without the aid or counsel of His other attributes, then He could be inconsistent, evil, and selfish.

What doesn't Sovereignty of God mean?

We do not mean that our decisions have been pre-determined by God. We do not mean that our actions are not our choices, but all are the result of God's previous planning. We do not mean that God makes us do what He wants in every instance. It is clear in our understanding of God that He is the perfect being and that all that we know about Him allows us to realize that how He operates is thousands of levels beyond anything we can comprehend. Some have tried to figure out how God makes decisions and planned out the universe and its history. The best they usually come up with is that it is all fatalistically decided, and we are ignorant of the decisions already planned out in the mind of God so make choices like you really have them. But this is not the vision of God or our lives that is present in the Scriptures. The all-knowing, all-wise, and all-powerful God is completely sovereign but has not reduced us to puppets. There seems to be clear variation allowed in the plan of God which is controlled by our choices (judgment on Sodom, David and the city of Keilah, Paul and the soldiers in the shipwreck). The God of the Bible is able to have a plan, allow limited choice, accomplish His plan, hold people responsible, know of other possible choices, let consequences flow from human choice, allow love to be real, redeem mankind, and allow individuality – all without being threatened as the Sovereign God. God is much bigger than any of us can imagine. Too often I find that theologians and philosophers want to figure out how all of this could happen, but we don't have the *being or makeup* to process how God does it – it's futile. Almost every detailing of how God is sovereign makes less than He is clearly revealed to be in the Scriptures. Be careful arguing about God using our finite limitations and in those ways distorting the wonder of the Living God.

Many Christians know this tension as the predestination and free will tension. The secular world knows the same tension as the form and freedom tension. Both are largely intractable problems which are continually debated and usually end up diminishing one side or the other. It is better to realize that God spans both sides and is above, beyond, over, and deeper than any thing we can possibly imagine. He is God and we are not. There have been some brilliant discussions about these arenas, and I would encourage more of them; but they will all fall short of the wonder of God.

He is Sovereign

What do we mean by saying that God is "sovereign"?

John Calvin writes, "And truly God claims, and would have us grant him, omnipotence (sovereignty) – not the empty, idle, and almost unconscious sort that the Sophists imagine, but a watchful, effective, active sort, engaged in ceaseless activity. Not, indeed, an omnipotence that is only a general principle of confused motion, as if he were to command a river to now flow through its once appointed channels, but one that is directed toward individual and particular motions. For he is deepened omnipotent (sovereign) not because he can indeed act, yet sometimes ceases and sits in idleness, or continues by a general impulse that order of nature which he previously appointed; but because governing heaven and earth by his providence. He so regulates all things that nothing takes place without his deliberation. For when in the Psalm, it is said that "he does whatever he wills" (Psalm 115:3), a certain and deliberate will is meant. For it would be senseless to interpret the words of the prophet after the manner of the philosophers, that God is in the first agent because he is the beginning and motion; for in times of adversity believers comfort themselves with cause of all the solace that they suffer nothing except by God's ordinance and command, are under his hand." (Calvin's *Institutes of the Christian Religion*, Vol. 1, 199.)

What are the ways that we see God's sovereignty?

Christianity has seen two major evidences of God's sovereignty in the world: preservation and providence. There is no such thing as luck or chance for the Christian.

Calvin writes, "Not that it has been commonly accepted in all ages, and almost all mortals hold the same opinion today, that all things come about through chance. Suppose a man falls among thieves, or wild beasts; is shipwrecked at sea by a sudden gale; is killed by a falling house or tree. Suppose another man wandering through the desert finds help in his straits; having been tossed by the waves, reaches harbor; miraculously escapes death by a finger's breadth. Carnal reason ascribes all such happenings, whether prosperous or adverse, to fortune. But anyone who has been taught by Christ's lips that all the hairs of his head are numbered (Matthew 10:30) will look farther afield for a cause, and will consider that all events are governed by God's secret plan." (Calvin's *Institutes of the Christian Religion,* Vol. 1, 199.)

What do we mean by preservation?

That God maintains in existence all the things He has made with all their properties and powers. God's sovereign preservation is a separate activity of God apart from creation. Creation brought the world into existence and preservation sustains its existence. The ancients all taught this physics principle that God's physical world points back to Him as creator but also as sustainer. There will always be places where we do not understand.

What is the proof of God's preservation?

No piece of matter has the property of self-existence or self-sustenance in itself. Matter does not have in itself the cause of its own being. Notice what Scripture states:

Nehemiah 9:6 - *You alone art the Lord. You have made the heavens, The heaven of heavens with all their host, The earth and all that is on it, The seas and all that is in them. You give life to all of them. And the heavenly host bows down before You.*

Colossians 1:17 - *He is before all things, and in Him all things hold together.*

Hebrews 1:3 - *And He is the radiance of His glory and the exact representation of His nature, and upholds all things by the word of His power. When He had made purification of sins, He sat down at the right hand of the Majesty on high.*

Psalm 104:29 - *You hide Your face, they are dismayed; You take away their spirit, they expire, And return to their dust.*

Psalm 36:6 - *Your righteousness is like the mountains of God; Your judgments are like a great deep. O LORD, You preserve man and beast.*

Job 7:7 - *Remember that my life is but breath, My eye will not again see good.*

Acts 17:28 - *For in Him we live and move and exist, as even some of your own poets have said, For we also are His children.*

Proverbs 2:8 - *Guarding the paths of justice, And He preserves the way of His godly ones.*

John 10:28 - *And I give eternal life to them, and they will never perish; and no one shall snatch them out of My hand.*

John Calvin writes, "Moreover, to make God a momentary Creator, who once for all finished his work, would be cold and barren, and we must differ from profane men especially in that we see the presence of divine power shining as much in the continuing state of the universe as in its inception." (Calvin's *Institutes of the Christian Religion*, Vol. 1, 198.)

How does God preserve his creation?

The only reasonable answer can be that He preserves His creation in various ways, many of which we are only now beginning to discover. Some we will never discover. The following theories have been advanced as to the *how* of God's preservation in different areas.

The Wound-Up Clock Theory (Deism)

God has left certain natural laws in place to sustain His creation.

The Continuous Creation Theory

God is continually creating the universe over again or at least is continually supplying the universe with new creation.

The Concursus Theory

This theory states that God concurs in all the operations of matter and of mind. Though God's will is not the only force in the universe, nothing without his concurrence could exist or act. It is important to note that all is not miracle or God's direct intervention, nor is it all mechanistic and God has walked away. Neither is God the ceaseless meddler.

All three theories fail when they try to be an explanation of the whole; however, they each might adequately explain a part of God's preservation.

What may be said about God's preservation?

1. God supplies all that His creatures need.

2. If God has not supplied it, you don't need it. You wasted it. You don't need it yet.

3. I realize that if I have a need, then somewhere around me God has already answered.

4. If I realize that I am going to have a need, then I begin praying for God to meet it and for me to recognize it. God has never failed on this plan.

5. God gives us an example of unselective compassion by the things He supplies even to those who hate and reject Him.

But I say to you, love your enemies, and pray for those who persecute you in order that you may be sons of your Father who is in heaven; for He causes His sun to rise on the evil and the good, and sends rain on the righteous and the unrighteous. For if you love those who love you, what reward have you? Do not even the tax gatherers do the same? And if you greet your brothers only, what do you do more than others? Do not even the Gentiles do the same? Therefore you are to be perfect, as your heavenly Father is perfect. (Matthew 5:44-48)

We are not being like Him when we only love and respect those who are nice and supportive of us.

6. **God many times supplies the component parts of the solution desiring us to put the pieces together and utilize them to deal with a situation.** He wants us to have the joy of the final assembly or the disappointment of the collapse of what we wanted because of irresponsibility. *I can do all things through Him who strengthens me* (Philippians 4:13). He may supply people, raw materials, counsel, time, and other things; and we must combine them.

God's preservation is sufficient for any problem.

There is no problem in which God's preservation cannot sustain us. Often we reject God's preservation and seek to handle it on our own and then problems become too big for us. Sometimes pride will not let us accept God's provision. It is also true that sometimes God's provision comes wrapped in a person we would rather not deal with. Therefore God has offered to meet our needs in a double wrapper in which the solution to one problem forces us to face another problem, such as bitterness or a clear conscience.

God sometimes preserves in different ways than we would like. When a person is sick, they may wish to be well; but God preserves them in the sickness with an extra measure of grace. This type of preservation is clearly given in the Apostle Paul's case of the thorn in the flesh:

Concerning this I entreated the Lord three times that it might depart from me. And He has said to me, "My grace is sufficient for you, for power is perfected in weakness." Most gladly, therefore, I will rather boast about my weaknesses, that the power of Christ may dwell in me. Therefore I am well content with weaknesses, with insults, with distresses, with persecutions, with difficulties, for Christ's sake; for when I am weak, then I am strong.
(2 Corinthians 12:8-10).

God's provision is often overlooked because of its regularity and, therefore, ungratefulness can develop. It is just as much God's provision if it comes through unexpected or miraculous means as if it comes through normal and expected channels – things like paychecks, jobs, bonuses, expected gifts. He deserves the credit and the glory for meeting my needs. We must acknowledge the person or agency through which God supplies, but let us not forget God.

What do we mean by the Providence of God?

The second part of the Sovereignty of God is His Providence. When properly understood and applied, this doctrine provides for peace and maximum achievement in life. This lesson could be aptly called: *How to develop peace in your life.* Or, *How to become all you can be.*

The idea of *providence* comes from the Latin word *providentia* and the Greek word *pronoia*, which means *to know before or to have foresight.* It therefore can be said to mean *providing for the future, because of special knowledge of it.* The word has come to mean in theological studies: *the government of God over his creation – all that God does to make sure that every area of the universe works out for His purposes.*

It seems best to understand that God, through His own deliberations, sets the boundaries of our choices. He does not, however, make those choices for us. He does in many situations determine the events that often can and do shape those choices. It is not God who determines the choices that we make. It is He that determines the choices that we will be offered. It is clear that all people do not at any given time have the same opportunities, or choices. It is true that through correct choices we can significantly improve and expand our opportunities. But that expanding path of choices has limits and is offered by God. I do not have the ability to choose all the possibilities that I might want.

The following are obvious choices that God limits. These are offered so that we can see the limitations of our choices. It is not difficult to see that God limits each individual's choices in much more particular and subtle ways. Here are some examples:

- I may want to be the child of different parents.

- I may want to be a different gender. (Note: Even if you make an outward sex change, every cell of your body is still either male or female.)

- I may want to have a 220 IQ.

- I may want to be the Queen of England.

- I may want to run a four-minute mile.

- I may want to jump off the Golden Gate Bridge and survive.

- I may want to swim to Catalina Island from Los Angeles.

There are many choices we might like to have, but we are not given the power or the opportunity to make those choices. For right thinking people it is best to reason that we shall do this or that if God's providence and righteousness allows us to (James 4:11-17). We are not free in the purely classic definition of that idea. The only being who is truly free is God. We are constrained in all kinds of ways. We may be free to do evil at any time, but what type of freedom is that? We are at times, by God's providence, allowed to pursue a course of action that is encouraging, well-fitting, and prosperous; but we did not create or cause the opportunity, the energy, or the desire to go in that direction. So while we are "free" to do these things, we must understand that "hidden" behind all our freedom is the hand of God. This is a comfort for Christians. It is also a goad – for if God has provided an opportunity for you to move that does not violate righteousness, then to not go down that path is unrighteousness (sin).

There are many times when general righteousness would allow us to go in a particular direction, but God in His providence will not allow. It would be righteous for me to become a doctor; but I do not have the skill, the time, or the inclination to pursue such a course. There are other times when God's providence will allow us to move in a certain direction (sinful) but righteousness would constrain us. It is possible for me to physically harm those who stand in my way, but righteousness will not allow me to use this means of persuasion.

What was originally understood as God's provision for the individual moments of your history (because He already knew your history) has become in some theological circles His deciding what you will decide in all minutia. This is not the proper or a biblical understanding of the concept of providence. God has foreseen every choice we would be confronted with and made provision at each juncture to choose a number of different real opportunities. Each opportunity is real and the one we choose affects every part of our future. Certain bad choices mean only bad choices are presented to us in the future. Certain good choices mean that certain bad choices are not presented at all and that certain good choices are available that would not otherwise be present.

Think of life as a journey where every decision at a fork in the road means we no longer have available to us the opportunities and choices of the path we did not choose. God has provided for us at each junction so that we could choose for Him or against Him. He has even provided, at many of the junctures, three choices (good, better, best) for Him and three choices (bad, worse, evil) against Him. His providence allows, provides, and even at times withholds those choices available to us.

One aspect of God's government of us is His limitation of our choices. As stated, we do not have available to us all the options that we would want, but we do have certain choices. There are always choices, and we are responsible for which one we choose. The choices must be ultimately ours for we bear the responsibility. We are not totally free in our wills because we are limited by our finiteness, our nature, our past choices, and God's particular limitations. The paths that are laid out before us are few in number but the choice is real. Each righteous choice brings more righteous choices. Each selfish or sinful choice brings more selfish and sinful choices. We ultimately build the life that we inhabit. Galatians 6:7 is true: *Do not be deceived, God is not mocked, whatsoever a man sows that shall he also reap.* We are free to choose the choices truly available to us. No matter how small and insignificant the choice seems, it is really a choice. The God of the Bible is big enough, smart enough, loving enough, and powerful enough to contain the variation your real choices create and still accomplish His ultimate purpose.

God's providence extends to more than just our choices.

It is important to take into your understanding how far God's sovereign control extends. We are tempted to rebel when God makes a decision that we do not like. But when we have hardwired the futility of rebellion by the extent of God's providence, we tend to calm down and go along within God's limits. God has given us choices, but they are limited ones.

God is in control over the universe at large (Psalm 103:19; 1 Samuel 1:6; Daniel 4:35; Ephesians 1:11).

He is Sovereign over the physical world (Job 37:8,10; Psalm 104:21,28; 135:6; Matthew 5:48).

He has rulership over the animal kingdom (Job 12:10; Psalm 104:21,28; Matthew 6:26, 10:29).

Even over the affairs of the nations He is ultimately in control (Job 12:23; Psalm 22:28, 66:7; Acts 17:26; Romans 13:1).

God is in control over a man's lot in life (1 Samuel 16:1; Psalm 139:16; Isaiah 45:5; Galatians 1:15,16). He has already determined how good your life can be and how bad it can be. You can make the decision as to which part of the lot you live on.

God is in charge of the outward successes and failures of men's lives (Psalm 75:6,7; Luke 1:52). In most cases people can be much more successful than they are and/or they can be much more miserable than they are. The choices that they make determine where in that range they actually live. God determines the range.

God is sovereign over accidental and insignificant things (Exodus 21:1; Job 5:6; Proverbs 16:33; Matthew 10:30).

He is ruler over the needs of God's people (Genesis 22:8,14; Deuteronomy 8:14; Psalm 4:8, 5:12, 63:8, 121:3; Isaiah 64:4; Romans 8:28; Philippians 4:19).

God has factored in your prayers into His rulership of your life and the people around you. If you pray, certain things will happen. If you don't pray, then other things will happen (1 Samuel 1:19; Isaiah 20:8,6; 2 Chronicles 33:13; Psalm 65:2; Matthew 7:7; Luke 18:7,8; James 1:17, 4:1-4).

God in His infinite foreknowledge, wisdom, and holiness has decided the destiny of the saved and the unsaved (Psalm 11:6, 37:23, 73:24). His justice in these regards has been upheld by the perfections of His being, or it would never have been executed. He is the judge of the whole world, and He has done right and will do right.

God is sovereign over the free acts of men. (Exodus 12:36; 1 Samuel 24:18; Ezra 7:27; Psalm 119:36; Proverbs 16:1, 19:21, 21:1; Jeremiah 10:23; Philippians 2:13) God has given us the gift of limited freedom of the will, and yet His plan and purposes are never thwarted.

God is also sovereign over the sinful acts of men (2 Samuel 16:10, 24:1, 1 Chronicles 21:1; Romans 1:24,26,28, 11:32; 2 Thessalonians 2:11,12). Individuals make their choices and God weaves these together to bring righteous consequences and His plan together.

How can God not be the author of sin but have ultimate control over the sinful acts of men?

Look at these verses as the starting place for a brief discussion and some proper boundaries as we debate this area so fraught with potential difficulties. It is the Scriptures that must answer these questions and not a philosophical discussion. Look at the various Scriptures and sense the subtleties that exist in this arena. God has allowed the possibility of sinful choice in His perfect universe. He is not the author of it, even though He provided for its possibility. It is seemingly to provide reality to the choice and reality to the possibility of love and worship (John 4:24). It is the angels and mankind who authored sin and God who has corralled it.

Blessed is a man who perseveres under trial; for once he has been approved, he will receive the crown of life, which the Lord has promised to those who love Him. Let no one say when he is tempted, "I am being tempted by God"; for God cannot be tempted by evil, and He Himself does not tempt anyone. But each one is tempted when he is carried away and enticed by his own lust. Then when lust has conceived, it gives birth to sin; and when sin is accomplished, it brings forth death. (James 1:12-18)

For all that is in the world, the lust of the flesh and the lust of the eyes and the boastful pride of life, is not from the Father, but is from the world. (1 John 2:16)

God permits some sin to be fully exposed. (2 Chronicles 32:31; Psalm 81:12,13; Isaiah 53:10; Hosea 4:17; Acts 14:16; Romans 1:24,26,28).

God prevents some sins (Genesis 20:6, 31:24; Psalm 19:13; Hosea 2:6).

God determines the limits to which the evil and its effects may go (Job 1:12, 2:6; Psalm 124:2; 1 Corinthians 10:13; 2 Thessalonians 2:7; Revelations 20:2,3).

"The evil acts of the creature are under the complete control of God. They can occur only by His permission, and only insofar as He permits them. Though they are evil in themselves, He overrules them for good. Thus the wicked conduct of Joseph's brethren, the obstinacy of Pharaoh, the lust for conquest of the heathen nations that invaded the Holy Land and finally the persecution of the church, the wars and revolutions among the nations have all been overruled for God's purpose and glory. In these instances we can see that God has turned evil into good. This fact ought to induce us to trust Him to do the same with evil of the present generation." (Theissen, *Lectures in Systematic Theology, The Sovereignty of God*)

What is the goal of God's Providence?

God's providence moves to the goal of God's glory generally through the happiness of the creature (Matthew 5:45, Acts 14:17, Romans 2:4, Romans 8:28, Psalm 84:11). Even His reproofs built into the system of the universe are designed to show us the way to find joy and wisdom (Proverbs 1:22-31). Do I respond out of gratefulness to His providential goodness? What are the ways I could realize that God is being good to me in any given circumstance? Do I trust God to know what is best in my circumstances? What procedures could I develop that will cause me to rest in God and stop me from being critical of God's plan? God's providence moves especially to provide for a people of His own possession (Exodus 19:5,6; Titus 2:14; 1 Peter 2:9). Do I cooperate with His purpose to prepare me to be His child?

What qualities is He presently working on (Matthew 5:3-12)? How can I ensure that I am cooperating with His plan for my growth and development? God's providence moves all things and me to enhance and reflect God's glory (Isaiah 48:11). Do I go with the flow of God's providence to declare the glory of God? How am I enhancing the glory of God by my participation in His providence?

How do I take delight in the Sovereignty of God?

I will be unusually brief here because each of these discussion points could launch into its own treaties. But please explore the wonder of the scriptural answers and how God being ultimately sovereign over everything brings delight and calm to your world.

1. I can delight in the Sovereignty of God as He uses the laws of nature (Genesis 8:22). Marvel at how God invented and uses the laws of nature, the values of the physics of the universe, and the timing of the events to bring our universe to the place where you are alive at this point with a choice to believe and obey God. Because of our mechanistic focus on the world, we miss the wonder of the mind that set all the elements in place. God put all these things in place through His knowledge and wisdom. When gravity causes things to fall, take delight in God's sovereignty instead of cursing. Contemplate the anthropic values for all the various equations and realize that God wanted you to be here. Go back over the timing of your life and see how numerous coincidences had to come together to bring you to this day and these choices. It is not random. It is not luck.

2. I can take great delight in the Sovereignty of God when He has used and will use in my life direct intervention (Exodus 18). God is still capable of showing up directly in my life. Like when I pray for a new job and it arrives before the week is up. Like when I ask God for funds to move forward on a ministry idea and someone brings a check for that amount without knowing about the need. Like when we need a miracle healing to save a person's life and God does it. Take delight in the Sovereign God who can change the flow of history to accommodate the choices of individuals and who knows when He cannot.

3. I can take delight in the Sovereignty of God as He uses my past choices to teach me, reprove me, and direct me (Proverbs 1:22-30). God has built a universe that responds to Him and to us. When we sin and choose to do that which will harm others or self, then the universe responds by reproving us. God does not have to be directly behind each reproof or chastisement. The elements of life respond and reprove us. They tell us that selfishness, evil, and recklessness is not the way to behave. God has built in feedback loops in all arenas of life. Take delight in this kind of feedback instead of resisting the bad behaviors.

4. I can take delight in the Sovereignty of God as I watch Him use those in authority to direct, guide, reprove, and instruct me (Proverbs 21:1; 1 Kings 8:58). God can and will use parents, government officials, spouses, and church leaders to direct people towards God's will. The question is whether Christians will allow God to get His message through the authority. Too often people are unwilling to delight in God's rulership unless He exercises it directly. I have watched God direct me through teachers, parents, pastors, police, and others. God is in charge and He has intermediaries who get His orders to us. Don't resist but embrace what they are saying.

5. I can take delight in the Sovereignty of God as He uses inner checks and restraints to present options and opportunities to me (Acts 16:6-8, Romans 2:15). As a child of God He uses my conscience, internal promptings, peace, or lack of it to show me which way to go. God is in control of the whole world and wants me to enjoy an abundant relational life. This means that I must listen for His direction. He is never seducing me to evil. He is never guiding me to fear. He is not filling me with doubt. He is not manipulating me through lies. But He can direct me through His still small voice and a sense of restraint or block about a particular direction. God wants me to follow His clues so I will get life right.

6. I can take delight in God's sovereignty as I stay alert to how He is using outward circumstances to guide me into the abundant life He has planned for me (1 Corinthians 16:9; Galatians 4:20; John 10:10). God wants to guide me in the decisions of my life to fit into the best part of His will for me. He can and does use circumstances, timing, and provision to direct me. When God provides miraculous timing to point out a particular righteous path, then take it. It is never God providing direction to do evil, but it can be Him directing us through open doors, provision, "random" opportunity, and amazing timing. Realize that you live in a world where the ruler of all is for you and wants you to get life right. Yes, there can be messages in the circumstances of your life.

7. I can delight in the Sovereignty of God when He uses dreams, visions, and even special knowledge in the lives of biblical characters and myself to make sure that His will is accomplished (Matthew 2:13; Acts 16:9; 22:17,18). In the Scriptures we see that God uses every measure to communicate with men and women when they needed to know. If God needs to have you know something, He will communicate with you. It is unusual, but all of the means of communication that God used in the Scriptures are still available to Him. He is in charge and if your choice must be made in a certain direction for His plan and your future, then He will make sure that you know even if He needs to appear in a dream or vision. I have regularly prayed to God for a higher level of clarity regarding what He wants me to do. He has always given me more than enough information to know which is the right course of action. I have never had it written on the wall, but there was always clarity which choice God wanted me to make.

8. I can take delight and peace in being a part of God's overall plan and not the center of the plan (James 4:7-10). God is God and I am not. When I relax into the overall control of God, things are so much more peaceful and delightful. Too often we have this idea that because we can cause some variation in our world, we are really in charge of everything. We could not handle all the control being in our hands, but we think we want it. God is in control and each individual is a part of the plan of God. The part we each play is determined by God and our own choices at various crucial decision moments. Bring your ego down and embrace the part you have been given.

Submit quietly to Divine Providence. Take time to admire the way that all the details work out. Take a moment to contemplate the precise timing of the events of your life.

Realize the wonder of what it took to provide all the provisions and options available to you right now. In so doing, you will find the Christian secret of a happy life. When God provides options, we are most happy when we diligently pursue the ones He has offered. When we insist on an option that He has not made available and we fight against the Providence of the Almighty God, then we make our life miserable (Psalm 39:9). Do not murmur at things that are designed by Divine Wisdom. We may no more find fault with the works of creation. It is a sin as much to quarrel with God's providence. If men do not act as we would have them, they shall act as God would have them. God's providence is His master-wheel that turns these lesser wheels, and God will bring His glory out of all at last. Let us be content that God should rule the world and to acquiesce in His will and submit to His providence. Does any affliction befall you? Remember, God sees to it that what is fit for you is given to you. Make righteous choices in the situations you are in and in that way adjust your life but do not rebel against the lessons and roles that God is trying to teach. Realize that God's providence works out for our good in the end if we choose to love Him with our choices, attitude, and actions. If I clearly understand my options, then I can rest in God's providence. This idea is developed much more fully in Hannah Whitall Smith's book, *The Christians Secret of a Happy Life.*

Conclusion

The Devil wants to devour (1 Peter 5:8). God wants to delight (Psalm 37:4). Sometimes we spend too much time thinking, talking, and strategizing about the Devil. It is God we need. It is God we should seek. The goal of winning at spiritual warfare is to be free to delight in God. Let me review. Pray a prayer of pursuit of God the Almighty:

O Lord I want to delight in You. I want to contemplate the wonder of Your being. I want to praise the glory of Your existence. I want to know You more than I do. I want to have my mind shaped by the truths of who You are. Show me the aspects of Your being that I need to pursue at this point in my life. Bring new levels of delight to my relationship with You.

Aspect	Verses	Definition
His Essence: His makeup or substance plus all of His attributes.		
Infinite	Genesis 21:33; Isaiah 45:5-7	God has always existed and will always exist.
Self-Existent	Acts 17:24, 25; Exodus 3:14	God is life itself and does not need us.
Spirit	John 4:24; Luke 24:39	God is alive, invisible, is a person, and has no body.
His Non-Moral Attributes: They have the least connection with us as humans and are very unlike us.		
Omniscient	Romans 16:27; Job 21:22; 1 Samuel 2:3	God is all knowing and all wise.
Omnipotent	Revelation 19:6; Luke 1:37; Psalm 147:5	God has all power and all authority to do whatever is consistent with His nature.
Omnipresent	Psalm 139:7-12; Jeremiah 23:24, 25	God is present everywhere.
Immutable	Malachi 3:6; James 1:17; Hebrews 13:8	God does not change.

Conclusion

His Moral Attributes: Some would understand that our limited capacity for these attributes is a part of the image of God in man.		
Holiness	1 Peter 1:15, 16; Job 34:10; Leviticus 19:2; Isaiah 6:1-3	God is transcendent and pure.
Goodness	Exodus 34:6,7; Psalm 34:8-10; James 1:17; Deuteronomy 30:9	God is loving, gracious, merciful, and longsuffering.
Righteous	Galatians 6:7; Psalm 58:11; Romans 2:7; Romans 1:18; Romans 2:5,6	God always does what is right and rewards and punishes according to righteous standards.
True	Isaiah 44:8,9; Psalm 86:15	God is ultimate reality (truth), is true, and not deceptive.
Sovereign	1 Chronicles 29:11; Daniel 4:35; Ephesians 1:11; Ezekiel 18:4	God is in control preserving, directing, and containing.

Most people are fascinated by God but few are in relationship with Him. Even fewer of those who have embraced His gift of grace in his Son regularly push into His presence and enjoy deep fellowship. But God invites us through the apostles (1 John 1:1-3) to have our sins forgiven and a secure place in heaven. Come and learn how to praise God while learning about Him. This work has been thirty years in the making. I have used these praise exercises with all kinds of people over the years and the result is always the same – a deeper understanding of God and entrance into the joy of His presence. Each time I practice these exercises – whether individually or in a group – it is as C.S. Lewis writes in his *Chronicles of Narnia*, "Further up and further in." There is nothing like pushing into the presence of God.

God has explained himself adequately in the Scriptures for us to have a clear picture of who He is and why He deserves to be worshipped as God. Take delight in what you learn about God and interact with Him about these powerful qualities about Him (John 17:3). We are to enjoy Him and grow in His grace and knowledge (Colossians 1:9-12).

Far too many people have a naïve and simplistic understanding of God. They cannot delight in Him because they know so little about Him. They are amazingly uncurious about the Supreme Being in all of the universe. This fact alone is evidence for spiritual warfare on epic proportions. The more that we do to get to know God along the way, the better prepared we will be for the wonder of life free from the Devil's schemes. God is so amazing and this book has hopefully been a beginning of your delight in the Almighty God. As you have seen, He is far more than you would have expected.

Look up the following verses and bathe in the sovereign control of God: 1 Chronicles 29:11; Psalm 115:3; Isaiah 45:9; Ezekiel 18:4; Daniel 4:35; Matthew 20:15; Ephesians 1:11; Romans 9:14-24; 11:36; 1 Timothy 6:15; Revelation 4:11.

Conclusion

Because reason, ethics, and ontology demand it!

If the Lord were not sovereign, then the possibilities facing us exclude morality, withdraw certainty, and throw the world into a random survival of the fittest.

What is the Sovereignty of God based upon?

It is based upon the total combination of all His attributes and His wise, loving, merciful nature. His sovereign rule is not an arbitrary act of His will. He has not come to the position of control and exercises it arbitrarily. What God decides and the position of control He exercises grows out of and flows from the totality of who He is.

About the Author

Gil Stieglitz is an internationally recognized author, speaker, catalyst, counselor, professor, and leadership consultant. He is Campus Pastor of Hillside Christian Church, a mega-church of 4,000 in Roseville, California. He teaches practical theology at Christian universities and graduate schools (Biola, William Jessup, Western Seminary). He is the president of Principles to Live By, an organization committed to teaching God's principles in a life-giving way. He sits on the board of Courage Worldwide, an organization that builds homes throughout the world to rescue children forced into sexual slavery. He has been a denominational executive for fifteen years with the Evangelical Free Church of America and was the senior pastor of a vibrant church in southern California for seventeen years.

Other Resources by Gil Stieglitz

Books

Becoming Courageous

Breakfast with Solomon Volume 1

Breakfast with Solomon Volume 2

Breakfast with Solomon Volume 3

Breaking Satanic Bondage

Deep Happiness: The Eight Secrets

Delighting in God

Delighting in Jesus

Developing a Christian Worldview

God's Radical Plan for Husbands

God's Radical Plan for Wives

Going Deep In Prayer: 40 Days of In-Depth Prayer

Leading a Thriving Ministry

Marital Intelligence

Mission Possible: Winning the Battle Over Temptation

Secrets of God's Armor

Spiritual Disciplines of a C.H.R.I.S.T.I.A.N

They Laughed When I Wrote Another Book About Prayer, Then They Read It

Touching the Face of God: 40 Days of Adoring God

Why There Has to Be a Hell

The Weapons of Righteousness Study Guide Series

1. The Spiritual Disciplines
2. The 10 Foundational Doctrines of Christianity
3. Basic Spiritual Warfare: The Three Enemies and The Four Weapons
4. Closing Spiritual Doorways

Podcasts

Becoming a Godly Parent
Biblical Meditation: The Keys of Transformation
Deep Happiness: The 8 Secrets
Everyday Spiritual Warfare Series
God's Guide to Handling Money
The Four Keys to a Great Family
The Ten Commandments

If you would be interested in having Gil Stieglitz speak to your group, you can contact him through the website
www.ptlb.com

www.ingramcontent.com/pod-product-compliance
Lightning Source LLC
Chambersburg PA
CBHW032110090426
42743CB00007B/304